Everything Makes Me Prosperous

Everything Makes Me Prosperous

a memoir of hope

& redemption

Joseph Carlucci Adevai

Third Edition

ISBN 978-1-960378-46-0   (paperback)
ISBN 978-1-960378-47-7   (ePub)

www.JosephAdevai.com

Book design by Anna Hall

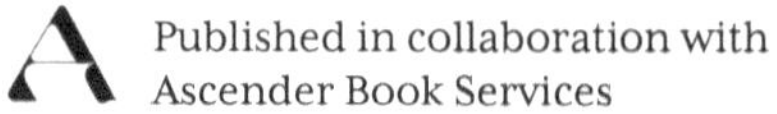
Published in collaboration with
Ascender Book Services

To Alicia, our children,
and grandchildren

Acknowledgments

First, I would like to thank God for saving me and giving me a new life. And I would like to thank the most important person in my life, my wife, Alicia, who has always shown me love, grace, and support.

To my children—Alexandra, Victoria, Jacqueline, Joe, Joshua, and Dominique—along with Alicia, you are the most precious people to me, and I can't thank you enough for the incredible impact you have had on my life. Your prayers, forgiveness, and support are what keep me going and pressing forward.

I would like to thank my editor, Kyle Fager—without you, this book would not have made it to press. Thank you, Anna Hall, for your amazing cover and layout design. And thank you, Stephen Knezovich, for your guidance on marketing and positioning this book.

Thank you, James Passaro, for helping me to get this project started. Thank you, Olga Vladi, for your editorial support. And last but not least, I would like to thank all of those people who have had an impact on my life, whether it be negative or positive, because in the end, it all makes me prosperous.

CHAPTER ONE

The Cat and the Kidnapping

I WAS ALWAYS my mother's favorite. For most kids, that might sound all right, but for me, it was a special kind of waking nightmare. I was born on October 31, 1959, and would spend the first years of my life in a ratty, crackerjack colonial with slanted second-floor ceilings and so little space you had to go outside to change your mind. That was the way it was for my family. We spent years following my mother's romantic whims around the state of New Jersey, always moving from tenement to dump to the borderline condemned. For a while anyway, we had each other, my older siblings and me. There but for the grace of God.

My parents met on a double date at the Hearth in North Brunswick. It would be like any standard love story, were the two of them not seeing other people at the time. My mother's husband was a man named Harold Dean, while my father's girlfriend was Harold's sister Doris. It must have been love at first sight, because my parents crossed over and had an affair that led to my conception. I would like to blame it on the era of free love, but the truth was, my mother just did that sort of thing. She latched onto men. Harbored obsessions. Really sunk her claws in.

It was in this way that the state came to record Harold Dean as my official father. My birth certificate even bears his last name—*Joseph Adevai Dean* was what it read. And it gets odder still. For a while there, my mother, father, and Harold all lived together in that little colonial on Oak Road. I'm not sure how it must have been for my brother David and sister Debbie, but then, they were only five or six at the time, so they probably didn't think anything of it. Harold lived in this arrangement long enough for me to start calling him "Dad." This is more than I can say for either my mother or my father, to whom I never felt close enough to regularly use terms of endearment. I always appreciated and respected Harold, and to this day I wish he had gotten a better shake in all this. He was a good guy, and the only person ever to give me a Christmas present when I was a child. He just got a raw deal.

I guess the last straw for Harold was when I got old enough for people to start commenting on how strange it was that I had tan skin and dark hair—the squarest of pegs compared to the rest of his fair, blond family. Eventually it became obvious to everyone that I wasn't Harold's. So he packed his bags and took David and Debbie with him part time. My father wasn't far behind, although he did remain with my mother long enough for the two of them to have two more kids together, a younger brother and sister for me.

That left me and my four siblings to make our way in a run-down place with an always bare pantry and under the care of a mother who was at times smothering in her affection and at times so distant we wouldn't see her for days. As a professor in the psychology department at Rutgers, she had a proper and intellectual job, but her true focus—her blinding obsession—was the men in her life. When she wasn't harassing the men she adored, she poured much of her love into me. Looking back, I recognize how this is the last kind of love you could ever want, but at the time, it was all I knew. She was my mother. And she had carefully manipulated us all to believe that she was the only person in the world we could trust.

I've never had the kind of constitution that would compel me to kill myself. My mother had different ideas. I can still see her there at that rickety old table, the pill bottle rattling in her quivering hand, the kitchen knife gleaming just to her right. In the memory, she's telling me how easy it would be, how much peace we would find if we just swallowed these pills, how there was no way out of our problems, save for this way. I was impressionable then. Twelve years old maybe. I didn't want to hear any of this. Didn't want to do it. Didn't want to be the hand she held as she crossed over from this life. But I was always my mother's favorite.

Let me back up. I'm always jumping to the end. What matters here isn't that I sat at that table with my mother, head in my hands, and nearly took those pills. What matters is how I got there.

I guess I should have seen it coming. I mean, what kind of house must I have lived in if even the cat went insane? I always hated cats. Or maybe *hate* is too harsh a word; let's say I strongly disliked them. Whatever word you choose, there's no denying that they're lazy and ungrateful. Plus, they poop in a box in the bathroom. There's nothing normal about that. We had a couple of cats. One was a Himalayan Persian that lived better than we did. Another was an alley cat we called Rags. The usual stressors were swirling in our lives that day we learned that even cats can get it bad, and we were dealing with them the only way we could: retreating into the television.

My younger siblings and I were sprawled out on the dusty floor of our sometimes living room, sometimes bedroom, watching *Lost in Space*, when Rags padded down the stairs, his eyes wild and teeth bared. This wasn't the first time I had seen the cat looking aggressive, but it was the first time I had seen foam frothing from his mouth.

"Hey," I said to my brother Stacey, tugging at his shirt.

My brother was so engrossed in the sci-fi cheese that he ignored me at first.

"Hey!"

"What?" he snapped, fixing me with a glare before his eyes followed along the line I was watching.

The cat snarled unnaturally—a savage, uncaged thing.

"Something is wrong," my brother said.

"I mean *really* wrong," I agreed.

Rags began to pace to the bottom of the stairs and then halfway back up again, his wild red eyes never wavering from us. Our pet, the same one that ate better and more often than I did, the same one that slept wherever he wanted, the same one that defecated in the same space I defecated, was sizing us up. He meant us harm. I had no idea what to do. My brother was backing toward the far wall. My sister had gone white.

"Help!" I called. Normally a child might call out to his mother in a situation like this, but by then, I had experienced enough disappointments from my mother to know that calling to her directly might not produce her presence. She might not have been home, and even if she was, she was about as likely to help us as the postman. No, with a feral cat bearing down on us, a vague cry for help would be far more effective.

Maybe sensing that his time to pounce was fleeting, the cat finally broke from the stairs and stalked into the room. I had hated Rags for long enough to know his usual look. He looked like a cat. This wasn't our cat anymore. Something had happened. This cat was possessed by some vile demon. This cat's mind had gone.

When my mother finally answered the call, she proved no help. She squealed, panicked, and shooed us all up the stairs, where—fittingly—she holed us up in the bedroom, quivering in fear of a deranged house cat. This is when things got strange.

The cat started going crazy, bouncing off the walls in the hall and screeching in ways that sounded less like an animal and more like a miter saw. My mother bellowed and pulled us close, the four of us shoving together in the corner of the room farthest from the door. By the time the sawblade of a cat started clawing at the door, I thought my mother was going to squeeze my head clean off.

"We have to do something," she said as if understanding this fact for the first time. "We have to call the police."

Karen and Stacey nodded in that numb, zombified fashion of the terrorized. We were all very much in favor of our mother taking charge. We always were. On that front, she nearly always let us down.

"Who's going to do it?" she asked.

We all looked at each other in pallid surprise. Why was it a question who would go? The phone was downstairs; we were upstairs, locked in a bedroom with paper-thin walls and a flimsy, hollow-core door. Between us thrashed a tabby-turned-hellcat, all bristling fur, razor-wire claws, and hypodermic teeth. In any other household, there wouldn't have ever been a question about who would brave the mad, weird path to the phone, because it would be Mom.

In my household, our mother looked first to me, then to my siblings, her face full of wide-eyed questions. When all of us shook our heads no, she shined the briefest glance at the ceiling before finally finding her head. "Okay," she said, puffing up her chest. "I'll go."

We three children wrapped into a ball of limbs in the corner as our mother threw on a pair of thick jeans and a hefty sweater. She put on some shoes and then wrenched a pair of socks *over* her shoes. After wrapping a scarf around her neck, face, and forehead, another pair of socks went over her hands. She looked like a Sherpa on laundry day.

"I'm going in," she said, looking back at us like maybe she expected a fond farewell.

Quaking anxiety was all she got in reply.

I guess she must have made it, because twenty minutes of nervous sweating later and we were listening to the sound of male voices grunting in struggle with a squawking feline. I was the first to brave the door. When I opened it a crack, I saw two burly men wearing police uniforms and large mitts on their hands. They were, with a long hook, stabbing in the direction of the cat, which by now, in its erratic rage, had become something more like furry lightning. It looked to me like the hook was making little progress, and it didn't take long for the cops to agree.

"Back up," one of them said. "I have an idea."

When I saw them again at the base of the stairs, they were shielding themselves with the coffee table, using it as a movable barrier as they got back to flailing. They advanced on the cat, eventually cornering it and snatching it with the hook. We all breathed a heavy sigh of relief.

Then they took Rags outside and put two bullets in him. It kept me up a few nights thinking about it because, I mean, who shoots a cat?

Shootings weren't uncommon in the various terrible neighborhoods we called home over the years. Always in connection with my mom's desire to hound some man or another, we would move from the lowest of low-life places to places that were somehow lower still. By the time we moved from North Brunswick to Remsen Avenue in New Brunswick, my parents weren't living together anymore. My father kept his own place. I'm sure he had his reasons.

Most of my earliest memories of their relationship involve the two of them fighting on the lawn. By then, the marriage had become untenable, so they broke it off. At least my father did. My mother apparently couldn't accept the notion that it was possible for her husband to move on, because she would harass him in ways I still can't believe. She would have David and me spy on him. She would send him threatening letters and phone calls. She called his employer once to tell them that he was homosexual—and back in those days, even a rumor about being gay was enough to get you ostracized or even fired. So I guess it was only natural that my father would come around yelling and making threats.

The most vivid memory of one of these fights came on a day we had spent huddled together, freezing in the living room because we hadn't paid the heating bill. I was just enjoying one of those fleeting moments where a spell of shivering finally works and you feel momentarily warm when I heard his voice howling from outside. My parents said many foul things to each other that day, but my childhood recollection has censored the language.

"They arrested me!" he was hollering by the time we got to the door.

My mom was already outside, posturing, her arms flailing wildly as she screamed something incomprehensible back at him.

I think I was too young yet to be embarrassed by the notion that my parents were causing a scene in the yard. There was a light dusting of snow, I remember—the kind that, because it was so improbably cold, looked thin and grainy, like sand.

"How could they have believed I stomped you and broke your ribs?" my father wanted to know, his breath like a smoke-stack on the chilly wind.

"Because that's what you did!" she screeched, blowing smoke of her own.

He paced, his swarthy face warming over in disbelief. "Look at you!"

"Yeah, look at me!" my mother said as she gestured at her apparently alluring form, still slender despite the heavy coat she wore. Her replies weren't always sensible.

"Your ribs aren't broken," my father pointed out.

I'm not sure how that one resolved—or even whether there was any truth to my mother's claim that my father would abuse her—but that's how it was. As my father cursed and gesticulated and stomped back to his truck, my mother would drag us back inside spouting invectives about how we had to keep down and stay out of sight because my father had a shotgun. I don't know whether that was true, but I do know it terrified us and drew us ever closer to the woman who kept us in constant need and consistent fear.

My father was basically a stranger to me then. The only impression I had of him was the one my mother painted for me. He was an imposing presence during those fights on the lawn, and as the version of himself that lived in my head, he was a frightening person. My mother claimed that he never had steady employment. This might be in part because she was always calling his employers and telling lies about him. Either way, he mostly did odd jobs and worked as a mover. What was clear was that, even though he cared about us enough to risk his jobs, his well-being, and his reputation, there comes a time when any man realizes there are battles he can't win. Eventually, my father stopped trying to visit us.

We chose to move to Remsen Avenue right around the time of the race riots of 1964. As a member of the lone minority family in the neighborhood, I was the only white kid in my class. This was a frightening time and place to occupy. My classmates were so adept at intimidating me that they could even turn their threats into nursery rhymes. "White cracker, white cracker, you don't shine," one of the songs went. "Bet you five dollars

I'll kick your behind." The rhymes weren't empty either. They would beat me up all the time. It led me to become quite gifted at changing my routes home, sneaking through yards and alleys instead of walking the sidewalks, and keeping quiet in class. I tried not to answer questions, even when the teachers called on me, because I knew if I spoke a word, I would pay for it later.

At home, I stayed home. There was no sense in venturing out of the house, day or night. There was just too much racial tension at the time, and to begin with, the neighborhood wasn't the safest anyway. That didn't always stop the trouble from coming to us, though. Those rare times when we had food, people would walk right in and take it. Once, some people threw a dead fish through our window, I guess as a thinly veiled threat about the Jewish look we had about us. We weren't practicing Jews, but that didn't seem to matter.

There was a camp across the street, all rotting wood and bright cloth and old trinkets. Before I saw that camp, I had no idea what a Gypsy was, but we wouldn't live in that neighborhood long before I got plenty familiar with them. It wasn't an intentional run-in that brought us together—at least not on my part. I guess my little brother Stacey was just too pretty to ignore. Rightly or wrongly, the Gypsies in my neighborhood had developed a reputation for taking things that didn't belong to them. They treated the world like one communal free-for-all. If you weren't actively using it, or it wasn't nailed to the floor, they would help themselves to it. One day, I learned that this practice applied to human beings, as well.

Stacey was about three at the time. His beauty extended well beyond cuteness, mostly because of his enormous and arrestingly blue eyes. Since we were almost always unsupervised as we played in the dirt plot that passed for our yard, people would often just come up and marvel at my brother.

"Oh, what an adorable little boy," they would say—even the ones that hated us to the point they would steal our food or make violent gestures in the direction of our house.

"Cute kid," others would say, a little more tersely.

I guess it doesn't matter what kind of neighborhood you live in; beauty gets appreciated everywhere, and by everyone.

Especially Gypsies, as it turns out. The Gypsies from across the street were particular fans of Stacey's eyes. They would come over and marvel at him nearly every time we worked up the courage to brave the outside world. Many times, they would just stand in huddles and kind of leer at him. For a kid—and for a poor kid most of all—sifting through dirt can be a riot of a good time, but sifting through dirt is less fun when you have an unwelcome audience. Sometimes, that audience would want to join the action, too. They would sort of inch-and-flank their way closer to Stacey, moving almost like a pack of wild dogs. Then, the moment one of us spotted them, they would shift to fawning and cooing over my brother. They would put their hands on him to the point where it made us all uncomfortable.

Then one day, I was in the house making a ketchup sandwich when my mother burst through the door, her face pale and searching.

"Where's Stacey?" she asked, sounding nervous.

We all started hunting. Stacey had a way of finding a corner somewhere and just playing quietly with whatever household item most resembled a proper toy to him that day. But after checking all his usual haunts, we realized he was gone.

"Where could he be?" my mother was asking as she paced around, pulling at her hair. She had assumed that glassy-eyed look that had become more frequent in those days. It was unsettling enough to see this expression when the house was relatively calm, but on a day when our brother was missing, it unhinged us all. We started freaking out, stomping around and yelling at each other about nothing helpful.

Then our mother finally called the police. I'm not sure how, but the cops quickly discovered that the Gypsies had him. I'm not sure whether his kidnappers intended to leave with him—maybe drifting to another neighborhood camp or, who knows, maybe even another country—but fortunately the police got to them before they had a chance to do anything beyond swaddle him up in some bright cloth and pack him away in a tent.

I guess that was when my mother decided we needed adult supervision whenever she was away at work or on one of her trysts. On the question of who would serve the role of "adult supervisor," as was almost always the case, my mother made a poor choice.

We lived in a single-family home that had been converted into a two-family home. This doesn't mean there were two separate entrances to the place—merely that we shared the space with a pair of young men we called "the college kids." We occupied the downstairs portion of the home while Edwin and Carlos, a pair of Puerto Rican kids I'm not entirely sure were actually *in* college, kept a place upstairs.

This was my mother's idea of hiring a babysitter: "Hey," she would say. "Mommy has to leave for a bit. Go hang out upstairs."

I'm not sure how willing Edwin and Carlos were to have a scrum of small children invading their space at random points in the day, but I do know that, at first anyway, we *liked* going up there. Their apartment was cool. They had an actual TV—not that piece of garbage we kept where you had to hit it every time your show went to snow. There were couches and chairs and tables and a bed for every person who lived there. It was almost like a normal home, and to us, that normalcy was exciting. It was great hanging out with Edwin and Carlos because Edwin and Carlos *had things*.

Never mind that it wasn't the greatest environment for children. Never mind that Edwin and Carlos partied frequently, or that they had a black light and the dope that tends to come with those things, or that they must have been handsome, charming guys because they never had trouble getting girls to share their beds with them.

It was fun for a while. But then Edwin took the party too far.

My mother wasn't home. I was hungry, but there wasn't any food for me, so I did what any six-year-old kid who lives in hunger learns to do to cope with the pain: I decided to go to sleep.

"I'm tired," I said to Edwin and Carlos.

They looked up from whatever seedy thing they were doing, their eyes bloodshot and their faces sallow and shiny with sweat.

"Why don't you go take a nap?" Carlos said.

"Yeah, do it in the other room," Edwin said all too eagerly.

I wasn't sure about the idea. I had my own room downstairs.

Sleeping there seemed like a better idea to me, but for the first time since the arrangement began, Edwin was adamant that I stay at his place until my mother returned.

"It's fine," he urged. "My bed is comfortable."

"We'll wake you up when your mom gets back," Carlos said before returning to his various indulgences.

So that's how I came to be in the bedroom of a young man who amounted to a total stranger. I hadn't been curled up long before I realized I wasn't alone. After the slightest creaking of the door, I could feel a presence behind me. I rolled over and saw that it was Edwin. Something in his eyes said he had changed in the few minutes since I saw him last. I never much liked the way Edwin looked at me to begin with—especially during those times when he had enjoyed himself enough to be all red-eyed and frantic. On that day, he had those eyes, but the rest of him was almost gentle. He eyed me up like a precious thing.

I wanted to say something, but I couldn't speak. As a young boy, I was too afraid. When first he touched me, I tensed, curling up tighter in an effort to shut him out. But then his hand slid over to my stomach, down to my thigh, and over my pre-pubescent manhood. I straightened up, clenching every muscle as if he might leave if I made a board of myself and pretended he wasn't there. I don't know how long he stayed, or exactly where and how he touched me, but I do remember a searing white fear causing my body to prickle and harden. I clenched my teeth so hard they hurt. My fingernails dug into my palms, leaving bloody scrapes inside my hands.

Then finally he left.

When I think about that moment in my life, I don't find embarrassment, even though this is the first time I've shared the memory with anyone. I don't know that I find disgust either. I feel only confusion—confusion and a sense of wonder about how a mother could possibly put her children in harm's way like that. But then, that was my mother: a desperate, selfish, lonely sociopath. There were only two people in the world she truly cared about at any given time: herself and whichever vile man she happened to be with. A possible third was me—but then, I was always Mom's favorite.

If I hadn't been, maybe I wouldn't have been so careful about preventing her suicide.

CHAPTER TWO

Careful Suicide

FOR THE MOST part, we were on our own from that point forward. This was generally fine as long as my older brother and sister were around, but they always went to stay with their father, Harold, on weekends. Every Friday, my younger siblings and I would cry because David and Debbie were the only sane people we had in our lives. I didn't even mind that David picked on me in those days. I always understood it. David was under plenty of pressure: being bounced from one house to another, always playing second fiddle to me with our mother, and dealing with the same sorts of neighborhood-related stressors we all had to face. It was entirely too much for a kid his age to have to deal with. David would grow up to be an atomic research physicist at Cornell. Then he would meet a Christian girl, who said that since he was a professed atheist, she would only date him if he could prove that God was nonsense. In his efforts to do just that, David found the Lord and gave his heart to Him. Now he's a doctor of theology.

Back when we were kids, where David and I often knocked heads, Debbie was like the mother figure around the house. Without her, I'm not sure how any of us would have survived. When I cut my hand on a piece of glass while playing on the mound of dirt behind our house, it was Debbie who bandaged me up and nursed me back to health. She was always protecting me and protesting everything else. Whether it was a call to flower child agendas or just a desire to get out of the house, Debbie was often joining sit-ins and demonstrations as we grew up. She would go on to college at Harvard-Radcliffe. Now she works in public health.

Somehow our mother managed to keep her job at Rutgers while obsessing about the various men in her life and generally ignoring the needs we all faced in our terrible home. I don't know where the money from her job went, because it wasn't going to food, proper clothes for her children, or rent. I know Harold was giving her some money, as was my father whenever he was working, but it couldn't have been enough. We were always on welfare and food stamps. We would eat government cheese. Sometimes our mother would cook us dinner, but she was barely around, so we were usually left to fend for ourselves. In addition to the ketchup sandwiches, mustard or even toothpaste sandwiches were not uncommon fare. I ate a toothpaste sandwich—for dessert, I guess—more times than I can count. Any time we had food that was any better than that, someone in the neighborhood would just walk in and take it.

It was around the time that I was in fourth grade that my mother started seeing Bob, a primordial-slime-glop of a man who lived in Franklin Township. My mother had a way about her, so it wasn't long before we moved to Franklin to be closer to him. The house and neighborhood were no better than the ones we left. Probably at my mother's urging, Bob would try to be a father figure to me, but that never worked out. Neither did her efforts to provide a father figure by occasionally hiring male college students to come entertain me and my siblings. It got so bad that I started inventing fictional father figures for myself. I pretended that my real dad was James Bond, the hero of the first movie I can ever remember seeing.

While all this was happening, we were living in a single-story, shockingly small apartment. The three boys in the family stayed in one room, while our sisters stayed in another. Our mother had her own room. The apartment complex featured some space to play outside, but the violence, drugs, and poverty in the neighborhood made that point moot. It was a pretty lateral move.

Just living close to Bob wasn't enough, however. Our mother also employed David and me to spy on him with these little toy telescopes. I'm not even sure where we got the telescopes, but I still laugh when I think about a pair of prepubescent kids shuffling into some ghetto-residential bushes to run espionage on a fat, pale, unattractive sleazeball of a man. And it was all because our mother was so cripplingly insecure that her constant assumption involved the men in her life cheating on her. In this case, it might have been happening, but we never obtained any evidence with our ridiculous telescopes. Bob was younger than our mother, and he had a sense about him that suggested he was just using her for sex. We got this sense because, often, when he would have sex with our mother, they would leave the door open. Whether in or out of the bedroom, the both of them made all of us uncomfortable.

Eventually I guess the relationship got close enough for them to at least talk about moving in together. We were all pretty shocked about it. Those conversations led them to finding a bigger house. Bob never wound up making good on his promise, but I guess that was to be expected. Either way, the next house did wind up being bigger and surprisingly decent. It was a middle-class neighborhood, which was new for us. Looking back, it's kind of funny to think that a move like that—one that should have made me happy and proud to be living in a proper home for once—actually made me more uncomfortable. We were way outclassed by our neighbors. My mother had a patient or two on the side of her regular job, so she was doing better financially, but it was still pretty clear that you can take the family out of the ghetto but you can't take the ghetto out of the family.

I remember a time when one of my friends had his dad drive him to my house to pick me up for a trip to get some ice cream. My friend trotted to the door and rang the bell. I saw all this happening because I was eagerly sitting at the front window—partly because I was excited about getting some ice cream and partly because I wanted to make sure I stopped my friend at the door so he wouldn't come in and see how we lived. While I waited, I had been hoping that his father wouldn't join him at the door. When he got out of the car and started following along behind, my heart sank.

My friend rang the bell and I leapt to my feet. I opened the door only wide enough to squeeze myself through. I saw him trying to catch a glimpse inside, but I think I got the door closed before he could see our dusty floors, our piles of dirty dishes, and our utter lack of furniture.

"I guess you're ready to go," my friend's dad said with a smile as he approached.

"Yes, sir," I said. I have no idea where I learned manners, because it wasn't from my mother.

"I just want to go say hi to your mom," he said as he whisked past me. "Just to let her know when you'll be back."

"No!" I said too loudly as I turned to stop him.

He looked down at me, eyes wide with something walking the border between surprise and concern.

I scrambled to think of an excuse for my outburst, and for preventing this obviously decent man from meeting the emotional rag doll who raised me. "My mom's, um . . ." I scratched my head, searching for an answer. "She's, uh, sick. She said to tell you she's sorry she couldn't meet you, but that you should have me home by, um, eight o'clock." Of course I made all of that up. My mother didn't tell me to tell this man anything. In fact, I'm not sure she even knew I had plans to go out for ice cream. Even if she did know, she wouldn't have cared about whom I was going with and when I was returning. This is a woman who routinely left me with total strangers. This is a woman who was always so busy dogging her men that she nearly got me raped.

"Oh," my friend's dad said with a pregnant pause. "I see."

I could tell he didn't entirely believe me, but to his credit, he must have seen that there was something more at work here—something entirely awful—because he pretended to believe me. In fact, he went out of his way to treat me with understanding and kindness, and to make me feel like I fit in, even with my shabby clothes and unkempt hair.

"Let's go get you boys some ice cream then!" he chirped.

I ran to the car so fast that I was the first to arrive by twenty yards at least. By the time my friend got to the car, I could see that he was already kind of uncomfortable. This would be the story with all my middle-class friends. Eventually they would come to realize that I was different, that my background lent me quirks I just couldn't overcome. It wasn't long after we moved to that neighborhood that the other kids quit coming around.

When my friend's dad unlocked the car, I slid excitedly into the back seat. My friend took his place beside me. They tried making conversation, but I was too keyed up to really contribute anything beyond monosyllabic confirmations that I did in fact understand their language.

"Boy, you really must like ice cream," his dad said with a laugh. "You're bouncing around so much, I can't get a word out of you."

"Wha?" I said, tearing my gaze away from the sights rocketing past the window. "Yeah, uh-huh."

When we turned a corner, the inertia caused me to topple into my friend, who, because he was leaning into the turn like most people would, shoved me away awkwardly.

"Jeez, Joe," he said. "You never been in a car?"

I could feel my face go red as I slumped and tried to hide myself by turning toward the door.

"You haven't, have you?" his dad said softly.

In a way, it was true. Not only was this my first trip for ice cream, it was also my first trip in a proper car. I had been in taxis before, but only rarely, and I had never ridden in a car where people expected you to buckle up and know how to lean into turns. This wasn't a public machine where you paid a stranger to drive you somewhere; this was a car owned by the person driving it, and because he owned it, he drove it with regard to his safety, our safety, and the safety of the other drivers. I had never been in something so arrestingly amazing. I'm sure it was just a standard clunker of a middle-class sedan, but the sheer size, power, and speed of the vehicle was about enough to make me leap from my skin. I loved being in a car to such a degree that it didn't even matter that we were going to get ice cream. We could have been bound for the dentist, and I still would've been jazzed.

In the rearview, I could see that my friend's dad suddenly felt sorry for me. My friend, meanwhile, seemed increasingly puzzled. I didn't let it get to me. The sensation of being included in the first place drowned out any discomfort my outsider status might have brought. As a boy with my lot in life, it was a remarkable feeling to be asked to go places. On the one hand, you want to go. On the other, you don't feel like you're good enough to deserve it. I was also twelve years old, so between the chaos at home and the puberty setting in, it was a difficult time for me.

My sister Debbie had it worse. She had just turned sixteen, and for some reason, my mother started taking an almost preternatural interest in her daughter's sexuality. I only know this because I had to serve as go-between on my mother's disturbing questions for Debbie. They always centered on boys and feelings and physical details I didn't want any part of knowing.

But then, not long after her sixteenth birthday, the questions started to get more specific.

"Do me a favor and ask your sister what she thinks about Bob," my mother asked me once. When she asked me these sorts of things, she was always terribly fidgety. That day, she was sitting on the floor in the corner of the living room, her hair disheveled and her expression askew. She couldn't seem to train her eyes on me. Instead, she kept herself entranced by the little game she was playing with her bare feet, where she locked one over the other and then switched them around. When finally, she looked up, she must have seen the resistance in my expression because she added the line she always added when she wanted me to do something for her. "You know you're my favorite, right? Can't you just do this one little thing for Mama?"

"Why do you want me to ask her about Bob?" I asked, that old familiar taste of bile coming to my throat like it always did when my mother talked about her increasingly distant lover.

"Just, you know . . . ," Mom said. "Just ask her what she thinks about him."

I didn't have to ask Debbie what she thought about Bob. I knew. She thought he was a walking sack of toxic waste, just like the rest of us did. But for some reason, I lied. "She likes him fine. Why?"

"She told you that?" my mother asked too quickly.

"Yeah, why?"

She looked away. "No reason."

That was the end of it. Several weeks would pass before I finally learned what the exchange was all about. In her effort to keep Bob from leaving her, my dearest mother was letting him sexually abuse her daughter. When I learned about the horror of all that, everything started to make sense: the reason my mother was growing more desperate, the reason David and Debbie were spending less time with us and more time with Harold, the reason Bob seemed even sleazier than usual.

I've still never reconciled the notion of what kind of mom could do something like that.

About the same time that Debbie started to withdraw from the arrangement, that's when our mother started threatening to kill herself. It crept into the routine as leverage for Debbie to keep letting Bob do things to her. My mother claimed that if Debbie didn't keep Bob happy, then she would take her own life. It worked for a while, but then I guess Debbie started to realize that if she didn't put a stop to this, our little sister would be next in line. In that sense, Debbie was a hero. In every other sense, she was a victim. We all were in our own ways.

For David and me, the victimhood came from growing up as sentinels tasked with preventing our mother from killing herself. We used to take shifts sitting or sleeping in front of the bathroom door, barring our mother from bursting in to eat pills. From the outside looking in, it might seem crazy that the two of us—such clear victims of constant emotional abuse—would want to keep our abuser alive, but relationships like these are different. She was the only mother we had. And she had poisoned our minds to the point where we believed everyone else was far worse. We didn't know any other way to live.

By then, I was living with a Grand Canyon of a hole in my heart. The other kids in the neighborhood had turned their backs on me, my older siblings were hardly ever around, and my mother—supposedly the only person in the world I could trust—was trying to leave this world entirely. It didn't help that I had to spend every night fighting for some semblance of sleep as I curled up on the threshold of the bathroom. And it was all because my mother thought some horror show human being named Bob was the very definition of her self-worth. Her sorrow over Bob forced her to the medicine cabinet more than once. Some of my most troubling memories feature the occasions when I had to pin my mother down and wrestle the pill bottle from her hands while she sobbed like a newborn.

That's when the miracle happened. Despite all the verbal abuse, all the nights he spent in jail on phony accusations, all the jobs he had lost because of my mother, my father started coming back around, trying to see us.

It didn't feel like a miracle at the time. My mother was losing Bob and seemed increasingly threatened by the notion that she would lose us too. If she was crazy before, you wouldn't have known it, because now she was busy writing a new definition of crazy.

Every chance she got, our mother would sit us down and tell us about how sinister my father was. She was smart, so she knew exactly how to paint the picture of the kind of monster a preteen would fear most. We learned he kept guns, that he hit the people he loved, that he couldn't keep a job or care for his children. It would be a long time before I learned the falsity of that. Even if my eyes had been open enough to recognize the phony little world my mother was creating for us, I wouldn't have noticed because I was too busy keeping her alive.

At twelve, that kind of thing wears on you. Makes you think there's logic in it. Makes you start to agree with the ravings of a sick woman.

So there I sat across the table from her. She had Tina Turner hair that night. Her eye shadow had run from all the crying, rendering her that corpse-like look of the already dead. And maybe she was already dead. She was breathing, her lips were moving, and the words were escaping, but from the sound of it, she had let go of life entirely.

There was the knife on the table. There were the pills in her hand. I'd already tried to wrench the bottle away, but that night, I had reached my limit on wrenching.

"There's no one who loves us," she kept saying. "It's just you and me, Joe."

And I believed her. I always believed her.

"You should do this with me," she said, her smile unnatural, pressed there in the center of her haunted face. "There's enough pills here for both of us. It'll be peaceful. When you die, you'll find real peace. Like nothing you've ever known before."

Peace seemed like a good thought at the time. I mean a *really* good thought. It was one o'clock in the morning on a weeknight. I was tired. I was tormented. I had been so sad for so long that I didn't know I was sad anymore. I had reached that point where you ask yourself if there could possibly be anything worse than this, and the answer isn't exactly *no*. When you live so poorly for so long, you learn that there can always be something worse. So instead, the answer to the question is something more like, "What does it matter if there's anything worse than this? This is what I have, and it's not worth saving."

If we'd been alone in the room, like we thought we were, I would have taken the pills. I would have joined my lunatic mother in passing to the other side. But we weren't alone.

David was lurking behind us in the dark. Listening. When I reached for the pills, he charged in and slapped my hand away. Struggled with me. Shot a hard, furious gaze at our mother. "Don't do it, Joe," he spat. "She's not worth this."

This was my brother. The one who took out his youthful angst on me. The one who was gone most of the time. I had thought he didn't care about me anymore. But then I understood he never stopped loving us. None of it was his fault—his anger or his love.

I remember locking eyes with him and being ashamed. So ashamed that I sank back to the table and put my head down. I listened to my mother and brother screaming at each other for a time, but I wasn't really hearing the words. There's a strange thing that happens to you when you have your eyes opened. For the first time, you see all the value in what you have, all the value you've been ignoring for sake of the pain, the fear. I sobbed. I wanted to apologize for what I had almost done, but I didn't know who to apologize *to*.

That's when I saw the knife. I sat back and caught the slightest glint in the low light. David had his back turned and was walking for the door. When he got there, he looked back at me. If he hadn't, he would have died that day. But I guess my wide eyes alerted him, because he sprang away just as my mother reached him with the blade. They struggled for a few seconds before it clattered to the ground and he shoved her away.

More screaming. More anguish. More desperation.

My mother kicked him out that night. And he was gone.

In many ways, losing my brother was far worse than losing my father. It would be a long time before I would see him again.

From that day forward, my mother would sit her three youngest children down on the regular and submit us to psychological techniques so dark I have a hard time acknowledging them. Carefully she shaped the notion that everyone and everything outside the house was dangerous and unworthy of our trust. Our father remained Public Enemy Number One, but now David and Debbie had joined the list, along with our neighbors, the police, the courts, and just about anyone else by whom our fearful mother felt threatened. It wasn't until later in life, when I took an interest in psychology, that I realized she was using her children in a sick sort of experiment. She wasn't raising us; she was trying to see what her mind games could do to us. We weren't her kids; we were her lab rats.

Having a parent who is trying to kill herself is intense and frightening enough. Having one of those and then also being told that everyone else in the world doesn't care about you, wants to hurt you, and wants to steal you away? That is an entirely richer sort of fear.

But this is exactly how, when the courts come calling about a divorce and custody case from your ex-husband, you get your children to lie for you, even if you're a monstrous human being.

It all started when the Middlesex County Court granted my father visitation rights. That first weekend he came to take us, we were terrified. I huddled in the living room with my siblings, our mother standing over us in her frilly coat, that grave look etched across her face.

"Now whatever you do," she said, her eyes darkening, "don't have fun. Even if you are having fun, pretend like you're not. And if he tries anything with you—" She looked directly at me when she said this. "I want you to run away and find the first taxi home. Do you hear me?"

We all nodded, and said nothing. This is kind of how we had learned to behave whenever she looked at us that way. Anything else provoked her ire, which in turn provoked more mind games.

The problem was that it *was* fun visiting with our father—or at least it should have been, had we not been ordered to have a terrible time. He got us some ice cream, introduced us to some half sisters we didn't even know we had, and even took us to the park. It felt like a proper family. It wasn't long before I started seeing Karen and Stacey breaking into the occasional smile.

"What are you doing?" I hissed at Karen when I had managed to pull her aside. The two of us were hiding behind the park's bank of seesaws.

"What do you mean?" Karen hissed back, the smile fading from her lips.

"We're not supposed to have fun."

Karen tried pulling away, but I held fast to her arm. "Mom's not here," she said.

"Fine," I snapped, letting her go. "You want to fall into his trap? Great. But me? I'm gone."

Looking back, it's difficult to imagine how a boy that age could have been so brainwashed as to not see the obvious truth. My mother had her faults, but she was certainly a compelling propagandist. The evidence should have been piling up right from the moment that I first laid eyes on his surprisingly decent house. Our mother had told us that he lived in a rundown trailer full of shotguns, so the firearm-free home had come as something of a surprise. Still, I was so convinced that my father was just buttering us up so we would let our guards down and he could hurt us that I actually ran away from the park that day. Because my mother didn't exactly explain how we were supposed to pay for it, I skipped the taxi and ran home instead. It was a long way. My lungs and legs burned by the time I reached our front yard. Strangely, the moment my shoes graced the grass in front of our house, I experienced the first sensation of safety I had encountered in more than a day.

That's the thing about identifying with a home of any kind. No matter how terrible it is, no matter how unsafe, there's still a part of you that takes comfort in the familiarity. I enjoyed my mother's praise that day, but in the back of my mind, my defenses against my father were already breaking down. He hadn't tried to hurt me. He had surrounded me with a positive environment and positive people whose smiles seemed genuine and not contrived like my mother's. When my siblings later returned home unharmed, this was further evidence that maybe not all was as it seemed. Despite the continued warnings about the dangers of the man who had sired us, I went back for several more visits. Each one proved more and more positive. I never ran home again.

It was around then that I learned the reason my father was able to visit us at all. The year was 1973, and as fate would have it, a law called no-fault divorce came into existence in the state of New Jersey. Prior to this law, one had to show due cause to file for and receive a divorce. Also, both parties had to buy in. Because my mother was such a controlling, vengeful woman, she had never allowed my father to divorce her. All this time, they were still married. I didn't know it at the time, but when I think back on it, it still blows my mind.

No-fault changed all that. On the day the law passed, my father finally got his divorce. Shortly thereafter, he applied for more frequent visitation rights. It was then that our mother really began to lose it. If I thought she was paranoid before, now she was like our cat Rags, all unchained, animalistic fear and rage. The closer we got to the court date that would determine our fate, the more desperate our mother seemed.

"You have to tell them the truth about your father," she said to me one night after she had finally let my siblings go to sleep.

I sat there bleary-eyed, desperate for slumber, and confused beyond reason. "What truth?" I managed.

Her eyes narrowed in that way they always did when she was trying to convince me of something a large part of me knew was ludicrous. For the first time, I noticed the unsteadiness of her hands, the clamminess of her skin. "When we go into that courtroom, and they put you on that stand to testify, I want you to tell everyone that he tried to kill me."

The need for sleep washed right out of me, replaced by shock. "*What*? He didn't try—"

"I know he didn't try to kill me," she interrupted. "But I need you to tell the courts the truth."

"What truth?" I repeated.

My mother didn't miss a psychological beat. "That he tried to kill me."

I blinked through my confusion for half a minute before I drew a breath to protest and was cut off again.

"I know it's not the truth," she insisted. "But I need you to tell the truth."

A part of me, even with as young as I was, knew that I sat in on another of my mother's mind games. Even so, the intense need for her that she had bred in me over the years continued to overwhelm my doubt. "I don't understand," I said, my tone revealing unintended acquiescence.

That hungry, victorious look crossed over her again. "I need you to *make* it the truth that he tried to kill me."

It took me a long while to answer. "I can't *make* him try to kill you."

That one seemed to stump my mother, who began some of her trademark pacing. "You're right," she said after passing some time chewing on her nubby nails. "You were always so smart." Then she stopped, and her eyes went wide as if she was realizing something for the first time. "You could lie."

"No, I—"

Before I could finish, she rushed in and clasped both my hands in hers. "What if *I* could make it the truth? What if *I* could make your father say he wants to kill me?"

I couldn't have been more confused if I tried. But in the confusion, I found my desire to please my mother and my need for sleep overtake me. "I can say he tried to kill you. As long as it's the truth."

The next morning, the phone rang. My mother was all too quick to answer. As I drowsed over a breakfast of off-brand cereal and water, she pressed the phone to her head only for a second before wildly delivering it to me.

"Hey, Joe," came the voice from the other end of the line. It was a male voice, but unfamiliar. It was gravelly and distant—a voice I had never heard before. "This is your father."

"Uh-huh," I said, flashing a sidelong glance at my overly enthusiastic mother. "What's going on?"

"I want to kill your mother."

The call was so ludicrous that I almost laughed. I would have, had I not been sitting under my mother's gaze. "Is that right?"

"If your testimony doesn't make me look good tomorrow," the voice said, "then I'm going to kill you too."

Sometimes a farce is so poorly executed that it almost seems like maybe it isn't a farce. Sometimes things look so limp and pathetic that you can't help but think that, really, only the truth could be so limp and pathetic. I was angst-ridden and old enough to honestly believe that only the truth could be so dumb. And if it wasn't the truth, well, my mother's expression when I hung up the phone was enough to make me believe I was doing the right thing.

"Well?" she said expectantly.

"It was my father."

"And what did your father say?"

"That he wants to kill you."

"And?"

I nodded, returning to my cereal, which by now was so waterlogged and goopy as to have turned into a chalky paste. I knew there was nothing even resembling the truth about that phone call, and I knew I was going to have a hard time lying under oath, but in the end, I honestly believed I was doing the right thing. *Sometimes a lie can serve the greater good*, I told myself, that little nugget of wisdom likely having come from my mother, master of lies. The truth was, I had decided that the crazy I knew was better than the crazy I didn't know. I would do whatever it took to protect the status quo.

The only thing that dented my conviction was when I looked to my younger siblings. By then, they had gotten good enough at burying their emotions to hide them from our mother, but after hearing me speak those terrible words, they couldn't contain the tears in their eyes. We all knew I would lie to help our mother. And it terrified all of us. But that's exactly what I did.

When the day of the custody hearing arrived, I was a wreck.

"If we lose this hearing," my mother told me that morning, "then your father won't just get you on weekends. He'll have you all the time. You'll never be safe again."

It was one of the lowest points in my life, that moment when I took the stand and lied about my father. My testimony was so halfhearted and implausible that I wasn't even sure if they believed me. And still, I did it. I looked at my father and said he told me he would try to kill my mother and me. I did all this under the serious pall of the lawyers staring up at me, the judge sitting beside me, and my older brother and sister and father in the courtroom to hear it all spill out. To that point, I had listened to all the testimony from friends and neighbors and family members, and it seemed that every last one of them was on my father's side. The things said about my mother that day were some of the same things she used to tell us about him.

From all the years of nonsense with which she had filled my head, I couldn't separate the facts from the fictions.

My younger siblings and I didn't have to go to court the next day, so we stayed home and waited around to see what would happen. Our mother was frantic that morning. When she returned home in the early afternoon, she was downright ragged. We couldn't get a straight answer out of her about what happened. Between our pleading questions, she was making phone calls—earnest, shifty phone calls about rides and arrangements. When we tried to talk to her, she pretended like we weren't even there. She was too busy, it seemed, to acknowledge anything beyond what she had to do. She had snapped out of suicide mode and into battle mode.

The next day, my father pulled up to the house around one o'clock in the afternoon.

"We have to go," our mother said.

We were all so engaged with the television that we didn't hear her at first.

"Your father's here," she snapped. "We have to go."

At first, I think we must have misunderstood her meaning, because we all rose dutifully, my younger siblings looking excited about the prospect of a visit with our saner parent. But one look at our mother said we had it all wrong. She was wild, her hair all sleepy frizz and her eyes sleepless red.

"C'mon," she said, shooing us toward the back door.

As she shoved us out, I stole a glance toward the front of the house, where through the front window I saw our father's car idling.

"Keep your heads down," our mother said.

Karen and Stacey began whining.

"And keep quiet," she ordered.

Stalking like prison escapees, we made our way through the yard behind our house, through a neighbor's yard, and to the next street over. There, our mother shoved us into a car that was already waiting for us. I had never seen the car, or the man driving it, but it was clear that this was premeditated. The moment she was in the passenger seat, she motioned for us to get low in the back, and as she threw a blanket over us, I remember thinking, *Does she really want us this badly? Or does she just not want* him *to have us?* I had been through plenty of territorial fights between them before. Once, they had literally each grabbed me by an arm and pulled me in opposite directions. Was this merely a more elaborate example of that same sort of vengeful rage?

It wasn't until later that I would learn that my sister Debbie had testified the previous day. She had said to the judge, "If you let [my mother] leave today, you'll never see those kids again."

No one ever said my sister didn't have foresight.

As the car started rolling, we were huddled so close that I could feel my siblings sobbing beside me. I didn't want to think about what all this meant, but I did know one thing: We would never see that house in Bloomfield again.

CHAPTER THREE

Crime and a Stunning Lack of Punishment

"I'M GOING TO set some things up."

That's the last thing our mother said to us before disappearing for two weeks.

She had brought us to this house in Staten Island to live with a woman named Beatrice. Actually, her name is a little fuzzy for me, so we're just going to call her Beatrice and hope I got it right. Beatrice headed a pretty standard middle-class family with two kids and a nice home. She was a kind woman, and she kept us well-fed, but that was about the extent of the joys to be found during this period of our lives.

The short of it is that we were terrified. We didn't know where our mother had gone or what she was doing. We didn't know anything about the people taking care of us. We didn't even have the full picture of why we had been uprooted in this way in the first place. This Staten Island was a strange and confusing sort of purgatory. The little I remember about it featured an emotional soundtrack of emptiness and loneliness. I had no idea what was coming next. Would our mother return? Would we be here for the rest of our lives? And perhaps most troubling: Would it really matter either way?

I think that's when I turned a corner emotionally. I was thirteen by then, a boy facing many changes, and a boy who did more than his share of crying. My siblings and I cried so often in that house in Staten Island that we hardly ever had time to talk to each other. Even if we had made conversation, there was nothing to talk about. We were stuck there. No school. No parents. No idea about our situation. We didn't even have any possessions, save for the clothes we were wearing that day our mother stole us away. I'm not sure how long I wore those same clothes, but it had to have been months.

"Where do you think she is right now?" Stacey asked me one day when we were in the backyard, doing the only thing we had available to us to pass the time: playing a game of catch.

The ball left my brother's hand and took a slow arc through the purpling dusk. With the sun setting behind him, I lost sight of the ball for a moment and had to duck away. It skipped past my feet, coming to rest in the tall grass behind. When I fished it back out again, it was slick from the afternoon rain still clinging to the lawn. I wiped the moisture away on my stained T-shirt and tossed the ball back to him on a rope. Stacey caught it with a thwack of the glove.

"How should I know?" I said, trying not to be as annoyed as I sounded.

"I don't know, Joe," Stacey said as he palmed the ball from his glove. He reared back as if to fire it at me again, but then something made him stop. His arm went limp, and even in the low light, I could see his shoulders heaving.

I had encountered this sight so many times by then that my response had become reflexive: I got all teary-eyed and quick of breath. "Don't, Stace," I said. "Please. Let's just have a catch, okay?"

My brother nodded through his tears, but I could see that there would be no putting on a brave face. Even as I caught the ball he threw back to me, I knew this would be one of the bad nights. This would be one of the nights where we would cry ourselves to sleep in our shared bed.

"What if she never comes back?" came the voice.

I gathered the ball in my hand and looked to Karen, who was sitting beside the plane of our game and picking grass with her delicate fingers. She hid her face, but the bouncing of her shoulders gave her away too. We were a mess, we three. The feeling of not knowing what would happen next was our constant struggle, but even that feeling was no match for the notion that nobody—not anyone and not anywhere—*wanted* us.

For two weeks, our mother left us there in Staten Island Limbo. She never officially told us what she was doing, but I've managed to piece it together over the years. Since she had effectively kidnapped us, she had obviously had to leave her job at Rutgers, so with all that free time, she was running around the state, working on ways to set up new identities for us. I can't imagine it's easy assembling the kind of people you need if you want to falsify birth certificates, Social Security cards, and produce any number of other fake IDs. It's probably also not easy assembling a phony story about a family background for your preteen children to memorize. But that's exactly what our mother was doing. How she could afford any of this, I'm not certain, but I suspect she was taking advantage of other people's kindness. Our mother was good at that sort of thing. My guess is that, upon finding out that she was going to lose custody of us unless she stole us away, she turned to a battered women's support group of some kind and leveraged their charity to keep us safe while she laid the groundwork to change everything about our lives and identities.

When she returned after her two-week disappearance, our mother was all business. My first thought wasn't necessarily that it was good to see her, but rather, that it was good to see a familiar face—*any* familiar face. Another positive was that I had never seen her so focused or intent on anything that wasn't one of her male companions. Whatever was motivating her, she was like a changed woman as she flew into our borrowed living space and sat us down to talk business.

"What have you told the people you've met?" she asked.

My siblings and I traded confused glances.

"Go on," she insisted. "Tell me what you've been saying to people."

"Mom, we haven't met anyone," Karen said.

This seemed to please our mother. "No one?"

"It's just been us and Beatrice and her kids," I explained. "We haven't gone anywhere or done anything or met with anyone since you left."

"Good," she said, nodding vigorously and folding her hands in her lap. She was sitting cross-legged before us, mirroring our own positions. She took some time to think, and then asked me a question as surprising as if she had smacked me in the face with a live salmon. "Joe, if you could pick any last name for yourself—any name at all—what would it be?"

"I'm sorry, what?" I said, furrowing my brow.

"If you wanted to change your last name to something else," she said, slower this time, "to what would you change it?"

Still young and naïve enough not to know what our mother was driving at, I puzzled on that one for a while. Growing up in so many different and such diverse neighborhoods over the years, I had encountered hundreds of intriguing last names. So many to choose from. I wound up settling on the surname of a friend from two moves ago.

"Carlucci," I said.

By way of confirmation, my mother spelled the name back for me.

I nodded. "I think that's right."

"Good," she said, rising. "Carlucci."

Then she bolted. We all got up to follow—all of us having about a thousand questions for her to answer—but by the time we found her talking to Beatrice in the kitchen, she had returned to that all business mode of hers. She didn't stay much longer that day before she disappeared again.

She was gone for ten days this time. When she returned, she was chock-full of documents and stories. Much like before, she sat us down in our borrowed room. There, in hushed tones, she started sorting through identification cards and giving us orders about our new names and how we were to comport ourselves around strangers from then on. Just like before, her focus was laser fine—sharper than I had ever seen it. Her paranoia, however, also remained in full force.

"Your first names are still fine," she said. Then she pointed to each of us in turn. "You're still Stacey and you're still Karen and you're still Joe." She gave me an unsettlingly large smile before continuing. "But from now on, any time someone asks you who you are, you tell them your last name is Carlucci."

I swelled with pride as I realized what had happened. My mother had allowed me to choose our new last name. It was the strangest and most unsettling gift I had ever received. Strange because how often do you get to change your last name? Unsettling because wearing a name that isn't yours feels a little like climbing into cheap motel sheets that clearly haven't been washed.

With our new names and backgrounds clinging to us—we were now the Carlucci family, formerly residents of a private commune somewhere vaguely to the west—Beatrice drove the four of us to a bus stop, where we took a ride to New York City and took up residence in Chelsea. The apartment was owned by a professional, kind, and flamboyantly gay man who lived in the building, as well. The fact that he generally left us alone was probably all my mother needed to adore him, given that she was still operating in such clandestine fashion.

The arrangement didn't last long.

"We have to get out of here," was all our mother told us on the day she uprooted us again and returned us to Staten Island and Beatrice.

It wasn't difficult to move back in those days because we didn't own anything anymore. We had left it all behind when we bailed on Bloomfield. When our mother came to move us somewhere, all we needed to do was stand up and leave. The clothes we wore were our only possessions.

Back in Staten Island, she found us an apartment to live in, but because the place wasn't furnished, we had to sleep on the floor. The thing I remember most about that place is shivering our way through the nights and starving our way through the days. Sometimes our mother would disappear for a while and return with some food. I don't know where it came from or how she paid for it. I just ate it ravenously. We did this for a long while before she finally seemed to piece together a plan.

"I think I've pieced together a plan," she told us one day.

We were huddled together in the corner of the hallway, where for some reason it was easier to fight off the hunger pangs. I guess not having to look at the refrigerator was almost enough to make you forget how much you wished something was in it. Anyway, there we were, looking up at our some-times-provider, all red-eyed and weak.

"We've got to get you back into school," she said, looking shiftily back over her shoulder. "Or else people will start poking around asking about you." She scratched at her head in that nervous way she often did. "We can't have that. But we can't have anyone knowing your real names either. Now tell me, what are your new names again?"

We all repeated our new names mechanically. She asked us to do this often, so by then, it wasn't hard to remember.

"Now I want you to remember that these are the names we're going to be putting on your applications for school," she said. "You have to remember never to mention your real name."

She went on to explain that she had cooked up this half-cocked concept that we didn't have traditional school and medical records because we'd spent our whole lives living in a commune in Pennsylvania. She'd had someone falsify a bunch of records from this commune, and even got around the need for birth certificates by claiming the place didn't draw any of them up. We got in based on phony records and false baptismal certificates from a place we'd never even visited.

I learned all of this in the interview at my would-be school, which is also the first and last place I ever forgot to remember my new name.

Mr. Unger, the fit, buttoned-up vice principal managing our application, pushed a piece of paper across his desk and asked me to sign it. By then, I was so nervous about not saying anything to step on the toes of my mother's lie that I didn't even bother looking at what I was signing—or remembering how I was supposed to sign it.

"Joseph Adevai," I wrote in my crystal-clear scrawl.

When my mother saw what I had done, she gave me the same look she gave my brother that night he saved my life.

The chill of terror swept over me. I'm sure I went white. I crumpled into myself. But then, out of nowhere—or out of the sheer animal instinct for survival that our desperation had bred in me—I came up with the lamest and most believable lie. "I was just joking around," I said with a half smile. "I always sign my cousin's name. I've signed him up for all kinds of stuff he doesn't know about."

The vice principal gave me a weird look—the kind of look you give to something sticky you find on the bottom of your shoe. Then he slid me another copy of the paper, watched me sign it with my true-fake name, and let it go.

So that's how I started my new life as Joseph Carlucci. That's also how I started high school. I'm sure everyone has trouble finding their youthful identity in a place where you're surrounded by hundreds of kids more experienced in just about everything. Now try starting that whole mess when you're a month late into the school year. Now try finding your youthful identity when the identity you wear on your sleeve isn't even real. Throw in the raging hormones, and you've got yourself a nice cocktail for a troubled teen.

Most everyone at my high school was Italian, which made sense since Staten Island was something like 80 percent Italian at the time. It was nice not to be a minority for once. That didn't mean I fit in. It's hard to fit in when you're living in constant fear that you might say the wrong thing and unravel the lie that is your entire life. I wanted to confide in someone, but I also didn't want to get my mother arrested, so instead of opening up, I closed myself off and embraced all the things a closed-off person tends to embrace—chiefly drugs and booze.

Staten Island was a nicer town than I was used to, but the crowd seemed tougher. Maybe it was the mob connections. I'm not sure. What I do know is that my friends were all a little rough around the edges. For instance, there was Dennis. Dennis lived in the projects. We met playing basketball, and were fast friends after that. He had been playing the outcast game far longer than I had, so it took me a long time to catch up to the way that kind of person lives.

Once, we were walking up the street toward his house, and we spotted a giant of a kid walking toward us from the opposite direction. The kid was at least a head taller than Dennis, and had to have had about fifty pounds on him. I mean Dennis was thin and handsome—not the kind of guy who looked like a fighter, but the kind of guy who looked like every smile landed him a new girl.

"There might be a little problem here," Dennis said.

"What do you mean?" I asked, trying to keep up as he picked up the pace.

Right when we reached him, the other guy drew a breath as if to holler at Dennis, but my new best friend just reeled up and jacked him in the face. Without a word or a move, the guy just wriggled to the ground and lay there, out cold.

That was Dennis. The kind of guy who would coldcock someone for no apparent reason. The kind of guy who would initiate gang fights just for kicks. The guy who introduced me to weed. The guy who introduced me to trouble. That was Dennis. He was my best friend.

I guess I identified with him because we wore the same bummy clothes. He had these purple Converse sneakers I can still picture to this day. Raggy jeans. Flannel shirt. Irish family. The guy lived and breathed the projects. Even so, I'd have traded places with him in a heartbeat. He had parents who cared about him. When we'd get in trouble, he and some of our other friends would say things like, "My dad's gonna kill me." Then they would look at me and say, "You're so lucky."

But no. I wasn't lucky. I'd have given anything for a dad who's gonna kill me.

Together, Dennis and I formed a group of eight or so friends from around the projects. We were tight, all of us—did everything together. Most of us were content to just sit around and smoke grass, maybe break some things once in a while, but Richie had bigger ideas. That's what drew me to him. He was a grand thinker, a young man never satisfied with what he had. So on Richie's advice, we started stealing things.

Give us credit: Right out of the gate, we aimed high. The first thing I stole after Richie and I decided we were thieves now was a Kawasaki 125 motorcycle. I just walked right into this driveway about half a block away, kicked up the kickstand on that beautiful bike, and rolled it back to the projects, where some of my friends and I stripped it down and repainted it. For a year, it was my bike.

Kid with a motorcycle, hoodlum friends, and a drug habit—I was playing out every Cool Hand cliché. School became more of an occasional pastime. As the year went on, I would spend more and more of my time at my house with my friends, where everyone would come to smoke pot and party. I remember we had this roll-up window shade that I would take down and spread across the table to prevent us from getting pot on the table or burning the wood with our ashes. With our window shade tablecloth, we'd get stoned and listen to Zeppelin for hours and hours. Then, when we were finished, I'd dust the shade off, roll it up, and stick it back on the wall. If your brain on drugs looks like a frying egg, I was facing a cholesterol-induced heart attack from all the egg-frying I was doing every day.

Call it a desire to have money for food. Call it a desire to impress women. Call it misguided youth energy. Whatever you want to call it, that summer, I was almost constantly compelled to steal. We robbed stores. We stole drugs and pills that we would later sell by a pizzeria. Once, we stole some lady's purse. I felt terrible about that one, so we never did it again. We passed our nights on heavier drugs like pure THC, blotter acid, mescaline, and Quaaludes.

By the time the tenth grade rolled around, I didn't bother going to school anymore after the first couple of days. I would often say, "I'm gonna go back. I'm gonna go back," but then, whenever I did go back, I would sit in the classroom and think, *What am I doing here? This is for people in society, and I'm not one of them anymore.* I identified as an outlaw. A hoodlum. That was who I was now. And it made me feel good.

This isn't to say that I didn't show up on school grounds every day. I would use the school as my new turf for selling drugs. I was brash back then. I'd sell the stuff right in front of the building, not caring at all when large crowds would gather around me to buy. Not even when Vice Principal Lipton—a pencil-necked, suit-wearing square who worked alongside Mr. Unger and doubled as a truant officer—started chasing me away whenever he saw me did I quit using the school as my staging area. Rather, clever as we were, Richie and I just set up shop near the girls' locker room entrance *behind* the school, where we could stare at the girls coming in and out while we smoked and sold. In a way, Lipton did us a favor. The view was much better back there.

That stopped after the school hired a security guard to stand watch over our new location.

If you're a mother, here's where lying about your identity so you can avoid prison comes back to haunt you: You lose all leverage over your sixteen-year-old son. It didn't matter how many letters about my absence the school sent, because my mother couldn't exactly call the police to drag me into the building. I'd have just told them my real name. So she was stuck. For the first time in my life, I had some semblance of control over what happened in my own home. Even when she saw me with drugs, she would have to just look the other way.

That's part of why I had so much freedom to do insanely stupid things. There was a Waldbaum's supermarket right across the street from the projects where Dennis and most of my friends lived, and despite its proximity to our hangout, we used to rob it on the regular. We were so brazen about it that, one Sunday afternoon, we cut a hole in the roof of the building, climbed down with a rope, stole a thousand cartons of cigarettes, and then spent the next week selling them outside a bank less than half a block from the Waldbaum's. I'm still boggled by that story. A thousand cartons stolen in broad daylight, and then we just strolled down the street to sell them in plain view of the place from where they were nicked.

We got so crazy about pillaging that Waldbaum's that we didn't even bother with proper equipment. Once, when we couldn't find our rope, we subbed in a garden hose. Everything was going fine until we opened the cigarette case and a brand-new alarm went off. The thing was so ear-splittingly loud that I nearly blacked out. Stunned as we were, we started tripping over each other trying to get out of the store.

"We gotta get out of here," my friend Angelo was saying as we scrambled for the hose.

"You're kidding," I said wryly. "I was thinking maybe we should just stay and listen to more of this sweet symphony."

Fast as I was, I got to the hose first and started to climb. But the more I climbed, the more the hose stretched. I couldn't get anywhere.

Meanwhile, joining the alarm bell was the sound of my friend crying and screaming. "My dad's gonna kill me!" he kept saying. "C'mon, Joe. Quit fooling around."

I don't know what it was, but I couldn't stop laughing. My friend's just crying about his mother and father and the trouble he'd be in if he got caught, and I'm just cackling like a drunken hen.

Eventually I got the hose stretched out enough that it would hold in place at least long enough to make some progress. It had to have taken me five full minutes to get to the top—my friend screaming and crying all the while—but we managed to make it out of there without getting pinched. Owing to that alarm, my ears rang for the rest of the day. Funny thing was that, even after we got out and stalked back to our usual haunt, the alarm kept ringing. It sounded off for four full hours before anyone did anything about it. The police never even came.

I guess it's a natural progression for thieves: When you get away with robbing stores, it's only a matter of time before you start thinking about taking down houses. Since we were so good at crapping where we ate, I decided we should pay a visit to this giant and well-manicured house only two blocks from the projects. And since we were such rocket scientists, Richie and I decided to rob it during the day. Now, stealing from stores is pretty straightforward because they're kind enough to post the hours of operation right on the front door, informing you exactly when you should arrive if you want to find the place empty. There are no such hours of operation on a house. You can break in and run into anyone at any time.

We cared little. That first house, we went in through a window in the back, took everything of value that we could carry, and bolted. There's a strange thing that happens when you find yourself in possession of a ton of new stuff that doesn't belong to you: You start to get the feeling that you probably should have taken more of it. Richie and I were just getting down to stashing our stolen gear in our usual hiding spot when he turned to me and said, "Hey, you saw those speakers, right?"

I nodded, open-mouthed. I *had* seen the speakers. They were big and new and cherrywood, and I could tell they were loud just by looking at them.

"You didn't grab them?" Richie asked, as if we'd somehow decided telepathically that carrying the giant speakers was my sole responsibility.

Any sane thief—one with a healthy fear of consequences— would just shrug and say, "We'll get 'em next time." I shrugged and walked back to the house. When I got back inside, I caught sight through the window of a woman in the next house over. Houses in Staten Island tend to reside in rather close proximity, so when I write that I caught sight of a woman next door, I mean that she was looking me right in the eye as if we occupied the same room. She was barking into the phone and gesturing wildly at the house in which I stood. Even through the two panes of glass that separated us, I could tell she was yammering at the police about the hoods she'd seen rummaging around next door. Figuring time was of the essence, I quickly hooked a speaker under each arm and bailed right through the front door.

No sooner had I taken a breath of the fresh(ish) New York air than I heard a screeching voice from behind. "Thief!" it yelled.

When I looked back, I saw it was the woman from next door. And she had an ice pick. I didn't feel like it was a particularly good day to get stabbed, so I picked up the pace. Even weighed down by the speakers, I easily outran her—but not before one last look showed her throwing the ice pick in my direction. It landed about a foot behind me, but the woman's intentions were truer than her aim. She'd rather see me dead than escaped. Laughing through the adrenaline, I left her in my dust.

Later, the police cars were out in force, trolling along the road in front of the projects. From my perch at the base of one of the projects' buildings, I saw that the ice pick lady was darkening the back seat of one of the squad cars. I watched as the police she was with got out of the car and entered one of the buildings. I waited in my shadowy hiding spot until they had finished searching the place. Then I snuck into the building they had just searched and hid there until my friends signaled that the coast was clear.

I can't explain what a rush that was. For a young thief trying to find himself, it was like getting high without the hangover.

It wasn't the last time I would have a close brush with the law. Robbing a bowling alley bought me a forty-five-minute pursuit by a police officer who was a surprisingly gifted driver and athlete. Even in his clunky squad car, he managed to match my maneuvers as I fled on foot. Then, after pulling into a driveway after me, he leapt from his car and caught hold of my foot just as I was climbing over a six-foot-tall wooden fence. I managed to slip his grasp, but not his ire.

Then there was the time when six of my friends and I relieved an office building of its printers and computers. That led to a scattering and a later rendezvous back at the projects. The trouble with chases like these is you have to worry about your accomplices getting caught. In my case, there was almost always someone who got caught. It took a while before any of my friends ratted us out, but it did happen eventually.

After my first night in jail, I was arraigned and released on my own recognizance. Since bad things always happen in multiples, just a couple of days after the incident, I happened to be wearing this stupid shirt with a cat on the back—the same shirt I wore when I robbed the bowling alley—when the surprisingly athletic police officer I had eluded on that occasion recognized me from the shirt.

"I know you," he said, his lips parting into a hungry smile.

So that was my second arrest inside a week. This time, they wouldn't let me go on anything short of $250 bail. I was sixteen years old and standing in court, lashed to a chain gang full of hardened criminals in for armed robbery and homicide, when the judge told me if no one bailed me out, I would have to go to Rikers Island. I was terrified, but what could I do? I didn't know anyone with $250. The judge might as well have made it $1 million.

That's how I wound up in Rikers, the only white person among hundreds of criminals getting processed that day.

Everyone else seemed to know each other. Meanwhile, I was the youngest, skinniest, and whitest guy in the place. I was convinced I was going to die. After processing, I found myself sharing a cell with an inmate who looked and smelled like he belonged there far more than I did.

"What you in for?" he grunted at me.

"Burglary," I said sheepishly. "You?"

His reply couldn't have been more casual. "Homicide. Bail's twenty-five grand."

I was scared, alone, and certain that something terrible was going to happen to me if I didn't get out of there soon. The food was just a notch above garbage. At one point, a fight broke out and shivs were pulled. The longer I spent in that place, the more I realized that I didn't belong there. I was surrounded by rapists and murderers and pedophiles. One inmate had been convicted of raping and murdering a woman before dumping her body in Central Park.

Eventually my mother did manage to scrape together the bail money. The moment I got out, I vowed to her that I would never let it happen again. To that point in my life, I'm not sure I'd ever seen that expression on my mother's face—that soft sense of relief for a loved one that only a mother can know. To that face, I swore that I would never steal again.

Selling drugs was easier and more lucrative anyway.

So let's recap. I was still in my late teens, and had already done a short stint at Rikers Island. On the day of my release from that hellhole, I took the ferry, then the train, and then the bus to get home, where I made an empty promise to my bail-providing mother. It's a strange thing, to look into the eyes of someone who has failed you so many times and tell her you won't fail her again. Her face went bone-rigid when I swore to her I would never return to Rikers. Her mouth fell open in that tired sort of look that suggests disbelief. She said nothing in reply, and I guess I can understand why. I think we could sense that our roles had reversed, and that both of us were at fault. How many times had she promised me she would come through for me when I was young, and now how many times had I promised her that I would start walking the straight and narrow?

Or maybe she gave me the silent treatment because she knew I wasn't done yet with living the life of the hoodlum. She was right, and it wouldn't take long for her to have her proof.

Less than an hour later—and I know people like to bandy about that descriptor, but in this case, I mean it literally; from the time I left my mother's house to the time I was standing in the trouble zone, less than an hour had passed—I was standing in a parking lot with a huddle of my friends, dishing out some weed, when the police paid me my third unwelcome visit inside of two weeks.

To be arrested for possession of marijuana within an hour of arriving home from prison has to be some kind of record. On that day, I don't remember feeling much like celebrating the achievement. I'd like to say that I experienced remorse over what I did, but as I sat in that crowded holding cell, watching all my friends' fathers come to pick them up, bail money in hand, what I experienced instead was a desperate sort of loneliness.

Every hour or so, my arresting officer would drop by the holding cell to see who among my little gang still remained. I guess he'd taken a special interest in us because we were so young. Or maybe he was just fascinated to see what the parents of a kid who could get himself arrested mere hours after departing Rikers would look like. Whatever the case, he kept turning up with his big eyes wide with concern, but his terse mouth all twisted into that look of parental disappointment I'd gotten so used to seeing from my mother.

"Hey, kid," he said to me once my gang had dwindled down to just me and two of my friends. "You made your call, right?"

He was referring to my phone-a-parent lifeline, so I nodded. I had called my mother, even though I had a feeling it would be a fruitless endeavor. She wasn't the most concerned or involved mother at the best of times, but that look she'd given me when I made her that promise pretty much haunted me as I sat in that cell. I'm sure that was her intention. For all her faults, she was always a gifted manipulator. Then again, given the fact that my promise had lasted a matter of minutes, who could really blame her for the no-show?

"If no one comes for you," the officer said in a grave tone, "we're going to have to send you back."

I could feel my face run pale. "Send you back" meant "back to Rikers." Even if my vow to my mother wasn't entirely genuine, I had at least meant every word of the part that had me avoiding further prison sentences. I might have sort of crossed my fingers on the promise to give up thuggish activity, but I had planned to do everything in my power to avoid going back to that terrible place. Everything except not passing around weed in public, I guess.

So there I was, really realizing for the first time in my life that you can't always unmake the beds you choose to make.

Another angry father came for another of my friends, and now it was just Biff and me and my lonely and empty thoughts about how very much I would love to have an angry father who would come and get me. Biff was sweating out the tongue-lashing he was going to get whenever his old man finally showed, but he had no idea how fortunate he was to have the opportunity in the first place.

In that moment, I resented him. I'm not sure if I resented him more for his ignorance on the subject of how amazing it is to have parents who care enough to get angry at you for getting arrested for possession of marijuana, or if I resented him more for the fact that his dad had the bail money that would prevent Biff from enjoying a stint with murderers and rapists. What I do know is that, when the cell door closed between us and I had to watch Biff walk away like a whipped puppy beside his fuming father, I'd have been overwhelmed with jealousy if I hadn't been so sad.

My arresting officer gave me another half hour of lonely stewing before he poked his head in the hall again. "I guess that's the last of them," he said, looking genuinely sorry for me. "You want to make another call?"

It was hard to keep myself from tearing up. This wasn't the first time he had asked me this question, but the song remained the same. There was no one else I *could* call. I shook my head.

"Okay then," the officer said. "Let's get ready to go."

My head hung low as the officer slid open the cell door. I had never felt so empty or afraid. I was so numb that I couldn't sense my heartbeat. It was as if my heart had fallen to my feet. The officer was kind enough to be gentle with my handcuffs. He even sounded disappointed as he told another officer that he would have to add me to the bus headed for Rikers. It's a strange sensation, caring for your captor, but in that moment, I liked and appreciated the very same man who I'd loathed for busting me just hours ago. I guess when you feel like you've hit rock bottom—when you finally realize that there's no one left in the world who cares about you—you grasp at whatever signs of affection you find, no matter how small.

"Let's get you to the bus, kid," the officer said. Then, leading with his square jaw, he walked me down the hall toward the processing area.

This hall bisected another hall that entered from the lobby, and just as we turned the corner, I heard a mildly familiar voice call out.

"Wait!"

I don't know what compelled the officer to stop, but he did. When he turned back toward the source of the voice, I could see a soft sense of hope in his eyes. I could hardly believe it when I saw Biff's father, his collar unbuttoned and his tie askew, striding down the hall with his arm outstretched as if willing us to stay put.

"Can I help you, sir?" the officer said.

"He's with me," Biff's dad replied.

The officer gave me a befuddled look. "*Him*?" he said. "But I just saw you leave with the other one."

"Well, it's a two-for-one deal today," Biff's dad said. In his voice, I could hear resignation, but it wasn't absent compassion. He might have been exasperated to have to bail out one of his kid's friends—and surrender the money besides—but he was clearly kind enough to care about me.

Either that or I was still just reaching for affection.

"You posted?" the officer said.

Biff showed him the receipt that said he had covered my bail. I'm not sure how much it was that time around, but it couldn't have been cheap, considering my record.

"Well, okay then," the officer said. He spun me around and worked off my cuffs. Then, as if stamping out any warmth he might have shown me up to that moment, he shoved me in the back and then gestured for me to get out of his sight. "Don't ever let me see you in here again, kid."

"No, sir," I said. And this time I meant it.

Biff's dad was awkward in manner on the best of days, but on this occasion, he was downright tongue-tied. He didn't seem to know what to say as he turned and invited me to follow him down the hall. An overwhelming desire to thank him came bubbling up from my gut, but my mouth just wouldn't follow through with the urge. I was too tied up emotionally to form the words I wanted to say. I had become a waif, just another piece of thuggish garbage to be swept into the gutters of Staten Island. And even in that lowly state, I found someone to care about what happened to me. My mother might have raised me in fear, my circumstances might have stolen my true identity, and I might have responded in the worst way possible, but in the end, kindness still conquers all.

I followed Biff's dad through the doorway and into the chill night air. The first thing I saw upon stepping back into freedom was Biff sitting in the passenger seat of a beat-up sedan. He was sniffling and rubbing at his eye with the palm of his hand. I don't know why, but seeing him cry made me want to cry too.

"Thank you," I finally managed to say to Biff's dad as we descended the concrete steps in front of the police department. "I mean it. For everything."

"Don't mention it, Joe," he said, though I could tell it burdened him. "There's hope for you yet."

The sentiment struck me as if I had just been slapped. I stopped in my tracks and slumped down onto the cold steps. Hope. It had been so scarce in my life up to then that it took me a while to remember what it was like. And for the briefest moment, I recalled its warmth. Then, sitting there on the front steps of the police department, I cried.

CHAPTER FOUR

To Escape with All That Cocaine

GETTING OUT OF Rikers aligned me with an opportunity to go to trade school on the state's dime, so I trained to become a mechanic. That's what I did for a living from the time I was sixteen to the time I was twenty. It helped a little with my positive-identity-building project—and it even fueled a little of that flickering ember of hope Biff's dad had given me—but in the end, I was still full of entirely too much angst. I worked my straight jobs by day, using my stipend to buy a 1966 Plymouth Barracuda, my first car. But at night, I made my real money selling drugs.

After grabbing my GED and starting at Staten Island Community College, I skipped out on the mechanic's gig and took up work with a pizzeria. The switch made sense for me, because selling drugs in and around a pizza shop was a natural fit. The trouble with selling drugs is that you wind up using so many of them at the same time. That's how I met my new friend, cocaine.

It was the greatest and worst high I'd ever had. On the upswing, I felt like I could climb a mountain in bare feet and then scream vast wisdom at the world below. But then when I came down, a knife to the head would've been better than the hangover. Like many of the world's greatest drug abusers who had come before me, I found the solution quickly: I just stayed high all the time.

Right around then, I left my fast-paced career as a pizza boy and started up the glamorous life of driving a bread truck for my friend Biff's dad. I worked the coveted 4:00 a.m. to 11:00 a.m. shift, making runs to Queens to pick up my hauls of bread and taking them back to Staten Island for delivery. Between— and often during—these trips, I would snort coke and party. More than half the time, I'd do my deliveries after not sleeping the night before. This period of my life was mostly a rage of gauzy days and weird nights.

One night, I was with friends at a club called the Paramount. Cocaine can bring out the rooster in a man, so it wasn't long before Richie—the grandest rooster of us all—got into a fight and pulled a gun.

"Richie, wh-wh-what, man?" Dennis said, flailing through the scrambling crowd to try to reach Richie before he did something stupid. "What are you doing?"

"Put the gun away," I suggested.

It was almost like Richie hadn't realized he was holding a gun in the middle of a public place until I said the word *gun*. His eyes widened with the gloss of understanding, and we took off. We careened through the hysterical crowd, everyone jostling for the exits. There was so much noise and so much contact that we got all the way outside before I realized that Richie still hadn't taken my advice. We'd upgraded from nightclub to crowded city street, and Richie still had his gun in his hand, just hanging casually by his side.

"Put the gun away, man," I hollered, grabbing for it. "You trying to get us thrown in jail?"

I don't know how we got into the cab of my bread truck without getting busted, but the next thing I knew, the four of us were doing lines off its various flat surfaces. Guns and cocaine have a strained relationship. They don't make nice with each other. That's why, when Richie started laughing at his gun, I knew our night was about to take a sour turn. I hadn't started the truck yet, but I was sitting in the driver's seat when it happened.

Dennis sat beside me in the passenger seat. Our friend Bobby was in the back next to Richie. And again, Richie's hand held a gun.

"Hey, check this out, Joe," Richie said, cackling. "I'm gonna—"

That's when the gun went off.

The noise was what struck me first. I had heard the thunder of gunshots in various parts of town, and I had seen gunfights in movies, but there is nothing that can compare to the sound of a firearm blast in a window-sealed bread truck. Whether it was the cocaine or my reverberating head, I wasn't sure, but my first reaction was to laugh about how Richie must have been firing blanks.

"Yeah, real funny," I said into the back of the truck. I could hardly recognize my own voice, my ears were so wrecked from the cannon that just went off next to my head. "Blanks are hilarious."

"No," Dennis said, his voice calm and even. "He actually shot me." Then he turned in the passenger seat and lifted his shirt to show me. The blood poured out of him in great gobs of slick red.

I careened toward a hospital I knew. I was so high from the coke and geeked out from the situation that I sped past two other perfectly good hospitals en route.

"Stop!" Richie said when finally we arrived at the turnabout in front of the ER. "Let me out of here." He fired a thumb at the still-bleeding but still-conscious Dennis. "You get him in there, they're going to start asking questions. I'm gone."

As Richie silently bailed, it was well understood that we would be lying to the hospital staff to avoid dropping any unnecessary heat on our friend. To his credit, Dennis kept his mouth shut about it for the first twenty-four hours or so. I guess when you think you're going to die, you don't want to die a snitch. But then, sometime after he found out he was going to live, he dropped the dime and Richie got busted. I don't blame him. I'd have done the same thing.

Richie should have been a constant reminder to me that continuing down the path I was on could eventually lead to something even worse than jail. At the rate I was going, someone was bound to wind up in a body bag. I don't know what it was about Richie—a natural magnetism for ridiculous behavior, I guess—but I always found myself getting into strange situations with him. Beyond the recklessness with guns, Richie just couldn't seem to figure out how death was supposed to work. And as high as I was all the time, I sometimes let him convince me that laughing in the face of it wasn't such a terrible idea.

The thing that Richie had that I didn't was a father who happened to be a police officer. So even after he got busted, he was out and free and living his life just like before. My friends and I were all hanging out at his place one day when a guy we called Beazer posed the question: "With all these drugs up here, why would you want to rent a room on the third floor?"

The place was your standard projects-based hole-in-the-wall. There was a tiny living room packed almost wall-to-wall with a secondhand sofa, which was in turn packed end to end with our burnout friends, all of them watching some old daytime movie on a flickering black-and-white TV. Adjacent to that was a bathroom just large enough to accommodate a stall shower, a narrow sink, and a rickety old throne. If you passed through the connecting door in the bathroom, you found Richie's bedroom—one of only two in the place, his parents occupying the other when they weren't at work. Richie's bedroom looked really lousy, with an unmade king-sized bed he had probably found a way to steal from somewhere, piles of dirty laundry, and various pockets of drug paraphernalia. It was the standard pad for projects kids like Richie and most of the rest of my friends.

On that day, Bobby had joined Richie, Beazer, and me in the kitchen, which connected to the living room on one side and the front door on the other. The four of us had retreated from the noise and the drug-musk of the living room to do our narcotics in peace at the kitchen table. At some point during the malaise, the subject of Richie's living room window—one of only two in the apartment, the other being in his bedroom just above his headboard—came up, and that's when Beazer and Bobby asked about Richie's choice of residential height.

"What?" Richie asked, his voice pinched from a full night and long morning of snorting too much snow up his nose. "What's wrong with the third floor? The view's nice."

A laugh came from the living room. One of our sofa-bound friends had apparently paused his bender for long enough to eavesdrop. "The view's of a courtyard in the projects, idiot," came the voice.

Richie shook his head dismissively.

"Seriously, though," Bobby said. "The third floor's pretty high up. What if we had to flee the cops? It'd be crazy to jump out the window."

Richie gave a look like he suddenly understood how right Bobby was.

I, on the other hand, didn't agree. "That wouldn't be crazy," I said. "A three-story drop is nothing." I don't know what I was on that day, but it wasn't cocaine. At least with cocaine, I might've had some sense about how stupid that thought sounded. But there I was, all high and brash about how dropping thirty-some feet to the ground wouldn't be a big deal. I honestly thought that if the police came knocking, I could leap from that window, land softly, brush myself off, and bolt.

"You're full of it, man," Richie said, cocking his head back in challenge.

The next thing I knew, the two of us were standing side by side at the living room window, looking down at the courtyard below.

"It's not that far," I insisted. "It probably wouldn't even hurt when I hit the ground."

"You want to put your money where your mouth is?" came the voice, this time from directly behind me.

I wheeled around to see that everyone in the apartment had stopped what they were doing so they could gawk at the potential scene. It was like they could smell the impending stupidity before I even had a chance to concoct it. Then I found myself saying this: "I'll jump out this window right now. It's nothing."

There was a great murmur of disagreement from the others in the room. Then somebody said, "A hundred bucks you won't jump out that window right now."

I had done dumber things for far less.

"Yeah?" I said. "Let me see the money." I might have been high enough to contemplate risking my life and legs, but after all, I wasn't stupid. Why give away something great when people will pay good money for it? That was my mindset back then, always seeking the cash that came with reckless behavior.

The collection plate passed, we had our prize money. Out I went over the ledge, with not even a second thought. I don't remember much about the fall, save for the compulsion to avoid the fence rapidly rising to meet me, but I do remember the landing. The crunch when I crumpled into the yard sounded worse than it felt, but it left me banged up all the same. Still, I was high, and I had money to collect, so I sprang to my feet and raced back up the stairs.

"Where's my hundred?" I said.

Grumbling, someone handed over the money. I was still busy counting it when another friend stepped in and tapped me on the shoulder.

"You know," he said, "you still owe me eighty from that last buy."

I slumped and handed over the money. Bruised feet, sprained ankles, and scraped everything else, and all I had to show for it was twenty bucks.

About a year into my delivering bread, the police impounded my truck because I had accrued so many unpaid tickets. I didn't pay much attention to the setbacks in my life back then because I was so busy selling cocaine. From my supplier, I would take a kilo at a time—which even back then was about $15,000 to $20,000 of the stuff—on credit, then sell it as eight balls weighing in at either a half gram or a gram. Nothing could have been easier. The only complication was that I needed a safe where I could store it because people were always stealing it before I could recoup my money. That and I was snorting so much of it that I would nearly always face razor-thin margins.

Around that same time, my grandmother died and somehow had some money left that she could pass on to my mother. There were about a thousand constructive things for which she could have used the money, but instead of any of those thousand, my mother decided to pour it into keeping open a bar called the Fairway Club. Her money management decisions always did tend to flow through her love interests. In this case, her boyfriend owned the troubled bar. Her financial investment didn't quite take the arrangement far enough for the boyfriend though, I guess, because my mother eventually found herself *working* at the bar, as well. It wasn't long after that when someone got the bright idea that I should come help out.

Normally I would have kept as much distance between me and my mother as possible, but for whatever reason, I decided that managing a bar would be cool. So I took the job, started recruiting friends and other young people to pay it visits, and even had my sister Karen out scouting for bands to play live shows. It wasn't long before the place became a hot spot for drugs and partying. We'd lock the doors at 4:00 a.m., but the party almost never stopped.

You get around all that success, all those drugs, and all that money, and it's only a matter of time before the mob gets involved. It was a typical evening. From wall to wall, people danced and drank. I slicked down the bar, my eyes bleary from the coke. Through the front door filed goon after goon in his twenties. I was no stranger to seeing large groups of men enter the bar at the same time, but these guys were different. They had a look about them—a look that said they didn't just own this place, but that they truly believed they owned everyone in it, as well. There were about thirty of them, and if there hadn't been so many drugs in the house, I might have called the police.

As the horde of goons made their way to the bar, I caught the eye of a regular I knew and flagged him over. "Hey, who're these guys?" I asked.

Just then, their apparent leader was sidling up to the bar. One look at him had the regular making a face like he'd just sat in something soupy.

"What?" I said, forcing a smile. "They mafia or something?"

Wordlessly the regular nodded.

"You serious?"

"Yeah," he said in a stage whisper. Then he told me the gang's name, which I'll redact here for obvious reasons.

Back then, the name rang a bell. I didn't know much about them, but I seemed to remember hearing that they were connected to a mafia kingpin out of Staten Island. As their leader took a seat at the bar and ordered a drink, his boys spread around the dance floor, setting up to sell drugs to my patrons. It didn't bother me—because, hey, drugs keep the party going—but their presence did kind of darken the mood in the place. A part of me had hoped that this would be a one-time thing, that the mob would move on, but then there was the other part of me that wasn't an idiot. That's how the arrangement went over the next few weeks. I would open the bar, Karen would set up the bands, and the mob would arrive to sell drugs to twenty-somethings who were already so loaded I don't know how they could stand.

About my new friends the mobsters, there had been word regarding their particular brand of justice. Again, for obvious reasons, I won't go into too much detail. Suffice to say that I never dreamed of crossing them, for fear that I might wind up disappeared. This is why I found myself sweating so profusely when, three weeks into the arrangement, a pair of them used that old mafia cliché of "Let's go for a ride" before shoving me into the back seat of a cramped little car. The seats were plush leather, I remember, but I didn't have time to enjoy the comfort with a well-dressed mob-shoulder pressing into either side of me. One of them had a pencil-thin mustache. The other had breath so foul it was all I could do not to wince whenever he spoke. Again, for obvious reasons, I won't go into more detail about their appearances than that.

"Listen," said Pencil-stache, "we like your club. We really do."

"Yeah," Rancid-breath chimed in. "But we're afraid for it."

I already had a sense about where this conversation was going, but as I turned away from my companion's foul odor, I played coy. "Afraid? What do you mean?"

Pencil-stache shrugged, the fabric of his fine suit roping against mine. "We're just afraid that the more popular it gets, the more attention it might draw from the wrong sort of crowd."

My eyebrows raised as I pondered what sort of crowd could be wronger than my present company. "I see."

"So we're thinking maybe you might want some protection," Rancid-breath said, and he said it in a way that made it clear it wasn't just a suggestion. "You know, to keep your place safe from unsavory elements."

The words *unsavory elements* brought with them a wave of syllables, on the crest of which rode a dose of awful breath that nearly knocked me unconscious. "Unsavory elements," I repeated, trying not to gag.

"Yeah," Pencil-stache said. "We figure all it will take from you is two hundred a week, and you'll never have to worry about any mafia types poking their heads into your business."

"Two hundred?" I snapped as I suddenly returned to my senses.

Mercifully, Rancid-breath kept his mouth shut as he nodded in reply.

"A *week*?"

Pencil-stache was apparently done playing games, because

he snatched me by the arm and squeezed. "You give me two hundred dollars a week or my robots are going to destroy that club of yours."

"Yeah," Rancid-breath said. "And we won't look too kindly on your family, neither."

There comes a time in every young hood's life when he realizes he's being shaken down by the mob. Two hundred dollars a week was entirely too much money back in 1982, but what choice did I have? I was stuck between a mustache and a gross place, and I didn't feel like waking up in a ditch that day. So I said what I needed to say to get myself out of that car.

Problem was I didn't have $200 a week to spare. If I was going to get out of this with my life and with my mother's latest boyfriend's bar still intact, I would have to improvise. Fortunately, when you do bad things as often as I did back then, you tend to meet people with exactly the right kinds of wrong connections. The guy I needed to speak with on this occasion was an acquaintance I made back when I was a mechanic. It turned out that this acquaintance was connected to a rival crime family in NYC. Back when I was still turning wrenches and carving out a path for myself as a dealer, he once told me that if I ever needed help, I should let him know. The kind of help he was talking about was pretty clear on that day, but we left it unspoken. But with the mob breathing down my neck, now it was time to talk.

I'm not sure what I was expecting to happen when I met with my mechanic friend, but I was startled by the ease with which he agreed to help me with my problem. I'd just finished explaining to him about my little encounter in the car and my lack of $200 per week to pay for my safety when he shrugged and casually said, "We'll take care of it."

"Excuse me?" I said, raising an eyebrow. I could smell the motor oil on his hands as he wiped them down on an oil-caked rag. The scent almost made me sentimental. But then I remembered I was a bar manager now. My life was on the upswing. "When you say you'll take care of it, you mean—"

"Don't worry about it," he interrupted. "Just know that it won't come back to you, okay? You'll never have to see these guys again."

I spent a couple of sleepless nights worrying about whether I'd just actioned a murder. Those two nights, it was tough to look Pencil-stache in the eyes as he patrolled my bar. But then, on the third night, a gigantic frame appeared in the door to the bar. The frame belonged to a notorious enforcer for my mechanic friend's brand of crime family. Immediately I tensed, fearing that this was about to get ugly.

Most of the crowd failed to notice the giant man shoving his way toward the bar, but Pencil-stache saw him immediately. I watched as his eyes narrowed and his face went white. The enforcer grabbed Pencil-stache by the collar and dragged him outside. I watched through the window as the enforcer slapped his prey around a few times in the alley out back.

For a couple days, it was quiet. The only mob-connected person in the bar was the enforcer who had cleaned the place out for me. Unfortunately, his justice had also managed to basically clean the place out of its patrons, as well. For a while there, it was just me and the enforcer sitting around in a place that used to be packed to the gills every night. Who could blame the revelers from dispersing, though? My friends from the mob were doing things like throwing M80s at the bar in their spare time. They made me plenty afraid that, as soon as my protection left, I would be killed.

As is the case with nearly everything, slowly the tension died down and people started coming back. I was the manager of a hot spot again. The next time I saw one of my old mafia friends in my bar, he had come as a patron.

"Why didn't you tell us you were with those guys?" he asked me, I guess waving the white flag.

Unfortunately, Pencil-stache didn't share that sentiment. Only a handful of calm nights passed before he returned, this time with a chip on his shoulder. He was clearly drunk or high when he took a glass off the bar and whipped it at this acquaintance of mine named Dominic. Everyone at the bar rocketed out of their seats. A great commotion kicked up from the dance floor. Before I could tell what was going on, someone had pulled a gun and started shooting in random directions.

I've seen enough movies about gunfighters to know the bartender usually survives, but I wasn't taking any chances with the people I loved. My sister happened to be there at the time, so I shoved her behind the bar to keep her out of the way of the violence. When it was over, I timidly looked around. The first thing I noted was the bullet hole in the wall right behind where I was standing when I heard the first shot. You might think that eying up your own brush with death might wrack a man' nerves, but to my great surprise, seeing that bullet hole imbued me with a strange sense of peace.

With all the calm of the Dalai Lama, I stepped out from

behind the bar and walked to Dominic, who was seething with the gun at his side. Somehow he had managed to not shoot anyone.

"Take a deep breath, Dominic," I said smoothly. "Calm down. Just give me the gun."

He was shaking with so much fear and rage that it looked like he had forgotten the language. So I reached out and slid the gun from his hand for him. Afterward, I felt like I'd really accomplished something with my life.

I'd like to say that was the end of my protection money saga, but six months after the initial shakedown, my mechanic friend's crime family started poking around and asking for a hundred dollars per week for protection. So instead of paying off someone I didn't know, I paid off someone I did know. Not even seedy bar ownership comes without its little hilarities. I would go on to meet mobsters who later landed life sentences, guys who would wind up dead, and even guys who would become the subjects of made-for-TV movies. They saw me as kind of a little brother, I guess. My mother saw them as an influence in my life with enough power to leverage me off my drug habit. She honestly called the mob to ask them to get me to kick drugs. Obviously, that didn't work.

The drugs had taken hold in my life by then. When I wasn't working, I would go from club to club and avoid sleep for days. Every Saturday night, I went to Studio 54, New York's most famous and infamous nightclub. Those nights would be full of glitz and glamour. And cocaine. But the in-between was a haze full of hangovers and wake-ups next to anonymous women and sleepless nights and almost no food. To others, I'm sure I started to look like one of those stereotypical cokeheads with the pallid skin, the dark circles under his eyes, and the starved build. In the mirror, I thought I still looked like how rock stars must feel. Once, I was at the end of a four-day sleepless bender when I passed out in the street. I woke up to find myself robbed. That was when I started hating myself almost as much as I hated cocaine.

Of all things, what would eventually send me careening back toward my downfall was my terrible driving record. I would get pulled over often, and nearly every time, I would get a ticket for having no insurance or registration. I would just throw the tickets in my back seat. One night, I was leaving the Fairway Club, my pocket lined with fifty grams of cocaine I had just scored from my new mob friends. That wasn't an insignificant amount of drugs to be carrying, as its street value at the time was $2,500. I packed my stash under the driver's seat and took off.

Ten minutes later, with the red and blue flickering in the background, I started to sweat out the sheer amount of illicit material I had resting on the floorboards of my car. The knuckle on the window alerted me out of my fear stupor, and I cranked the window down. I decided to kickstart the conversation with the standard line. "What seems to be the troub—"

"License and registration," the officer interrupted.

I didn't have either of those things, so I played my lips into a nervous little smile. "Funny story," I said, but he didn't let me finish.

Down at the precinct, I learned from my latest arresting officer that I had more than ten suspensions of my license. That night, they put me in a cell and impounded my car. The former was fine. I'd been here so many times for this same offense that I'd come to think of it as a kind of occasional flophouse. It was the impounding of my car that had me worried. I couldn't sleep that night because I knew my life was over. With all that cocaine in my car, I'd become just another poster boy for President Reagan's only recently enacted War on Drugs. Anyone caught with the intent to distribute—which is a category my stash of cocaine certainly put me in, even if I had meant to use it personally—would face a sentence of twenty years in prison. So I spent that night thinking that the next time I saw the outside of a jail cell would be sometime after the year 2000.

It was a long, tense night. A hundred times, I pictured the impound officers rooting through my car and finding the coke. I pictured them straightening up and smiling hungry grins. "Well, well, well," they would say in these imaginings. "Looks like we've got ourselves a lifer."

Every time I heard a guard's footsteps, I just knew they were coming for me. I would seize up, close my eyes tight, and try not to lose it entirely. But every time, those footsteps would walk on past. All night, no one opened my cell. The next morning, after a friend arrived with bail money, they let me go with a warning that if they caught me driving again, I'd wind up in proper prison. As a reminder, they said they were keeping my car.

I was thankful to have avoided Rikers again, but I knew the honeymoon would only last for as long as nobody thought to check the lifelong traffic violator's car for illegal substances.

I turned to my bailout friend and made him a solemn vow. "One way or another, I'm getting that car out of that precinct."

"What are you talking about, man?" my somewhat more sensible friend was saying. "It's in impound. You ever been to impound? That place is probably a fortress."

"I don't care," I insisted. "Whatever I have to do, that car is getting out."

Imagine our surprise when my friend dropped me off next to the impound lot and we discovered that it was basically just a parking lot. I was alone in this wide-open space full of cars as I hotwired the ignition. The police were even kind enough to leave my cocaine under the seat.

As I started the ignition and wheeled out of there, I found myself thanking a God I didn't even really know. Tears streamed down my face as I screamed through a combination of joy and regret. I could not have been more excited. At the time, I thought the excitement came from how narrowly I had avoided a long-term prison sentence, but looking back, I have a feeling that most of it was because I'd managed to escape without losing all that cocaine.

The truth was that I'd become an addict. I was thanking God *for* saving me, but what I really should have been doing was asking God *to* save me. In those later stages of my demise, though, I never would have allowed God to get through to me. What I needed was a father.

When I was twenty-five, I moved back home with my mother after being kicked out of several apartments. It seemed my landlords never much cared for how my rental spaces always tended to become coke houses. Managing the Fairway Club had become something of a drag, so I was in the process of looking for a regular job. My would-be girlfriend was also in the process of looking for a regular boyfriend. We had been dating for a couple of years, but I was never faithful to her. The dance was always the same. I would disappear for days; she would come looking for me; she would find me wrapped up in the body of another woman; she would smack me one.

Around this same time, I finally started to see the light on how addicted to coke I had become. I had started freebasing crack, which is about as deep into cocaine as you can get. It took a few experiences of blacking out on the stuff before I realized that, one of these times, I might not wake up again.

Looking back, the rapidity with which I managed to go on the relatively straight and narrow is alarming. In fact, it was downright easy for me to at least pretend to straighten up my act. I took a job at a bank in New York and got to work on reshaping an image of myself as a straightlaced working man. Meanwhile, I'd managed to kick the crack, but I was still too into the cocaine to let it go entirely.

Life at home with my mother was about as smooth as you might imagine. We'd put each other through several circles of hell by that point, so our conversations were always chilly. She had become something of a hollow shell by then, which made it easier for me to antagonize her. At the time, my favorite subject had become prodding questions about my father.

"What happened to my father?" I would ask her at random—and often in response to some form of nagging she was laying on me. "Is he really that bad that we had to lock him out of my life?"

I honestly started to think that my lack of a father figure was to blame for all my personal ills. I was really into shoveling responsibility for my actions onto other people back then. Despite her psychology background, my mother was never much help in getting to the bottom of my father issues, but coincidentally, my own bad habits would wind up breaking the case.

Of course, I never quit driving, even though I'd only just recently escaped a long-term prison sentence by the skin of my teeth and the grace of God. So when I was pulled over again, I didn't know what to do. My driving record was so littered with horrors that I knew I'd never get out of this one. Then, when I heard that old familiar knuckle on the driver's window, it came to me in a flash of inspiration.

I didn't have a license or registration to provide, so the officer asked for my name.

I knew that giving the officer my fake name, Joseph Carlucci, would make for a rough day. So instead, I tried a novel idea: I gave him my real name.

"Joe Adevai," I said. It was the first time in over a decade that I had said that name to anyone.

The officer nodded gravely, wrote me a ticket, and let me go.

I couldn't believe how easy it was. I shook my head, laughing at how many terrible situations I could have avoided if only I'd just thought to use this obvious trick earlier in life.

It would be a few days before I would learn of the second edge on that sword that was my real name. I remember I was sitting at the kitchen table, just staring through the steam in my coffee and at the wall beyond, when my sister Karen came running. I don't know why I was so dazed, but I suspect it had something to do with a hangover. It had been a long while since I had seen Karen excited about anything, so it took me a long moment to piece together what her expression even meant.

"Come quick!" she said, her tone not meshing terribly well with my searing headache.

"What?" I whined, annoyed. "What is it?"

"Some guy is here. Oh my God." She was hopping up and down like a child far younger than she was. I guess she had always been rather prone to histrionics, but it had been months, if not years, since I had seen her do a little dance like this one.

"Some guy is here?" I repeated as I rubbed the bridge of my nose with my fingers. "Okay, great. I'll call Tom Brokaw."

"No, you don't understand." My sister reached out and started tugging on my sleeve.

I clutched my coffee as if it was an anchor that would keep me from having to follow her.

"I think it's Big Joe!"

It had been a while since I had thought about that name so, coupled with the drug fog, it took me several solid seconds to put a face to what Karen was talking about. Big Joe. Who was Big Joe again? Then it hit me: That's what we used to call my father. My true father. The man my mother had taught me would kill me on sight. The man I had spent my youth believing to be a monster. The man from whom we had been running for years.

When understanding crossed my face, Karen's expression changed from excitement to concern. We were all still deluded enough to think that our mother getting arrested for kidnapping would be a bad thing, so I guess we both had that same dreaded thought at the same time. If Big Joe was here, what would that mean for our mother?

"Oh my God, what do we do?" Karen said, her dance blending from one of excitement to one of panic. The general steps were the same, but the tempo had picked up.

"I'll just have to take care of him," I said.

Maybe it was the screw-all sensation that comes with having a hangover, or maybe it was the thought of how much I had grown since the last time I encountered Big Joe, but whatever the case, I found myself not caring a lick about how horrible my mother had always said my father was. He might be big and mean and possessed of a shotgun, but I could take him. And if I couldn't, well, at least a good beating would give me something else to think about besides my hangover.

By that point, I hadn't seen my father in twelve or thirteen years, so I wasn't entirely sure he was actually the man parking the car across the street. My mood upon first stepping into the yard and making my way toward him was one of determined aggression. But then, as I drew closer to him, a strange new sensation took over. I was *hoping* that this was my father. There were good reasons for this. For one thing, what could he really do to my siblings and me now? We were all over eighteen. All adults. I had just been saying something like this to my mother several days earlier. But the more important reason that I was hoping this man was my father was that he might know how I could contact David and Debbie. It's one thing to go over a decade without seeing a father you hardly know and have been taught to hate; it's entirely another to go over a decade without seeing two siblings you dearly love. Being away from David, in particular, was the single greatest sorrow in a young life chock-full of great sorrows.

By the time I reached the driver's side door, all anger had left me. He pretended not to notice my approach until I knocked on the window. Then he startled and rolled the window down.

"Are you my father?" I said simply.

"Yeah," he said. "I am."

In the driver's seat was an attractive middle-aged woman I didn't recognize. She was smiling at me as if I had just arrived to fulfill a longtime wish of hers. Later I would learn that she was Pat, my father's new wife.

"So you found us, huh?" I said.

His eyes started to glisten. "You don't know how long I've been looking."

I looked back at the house as if I could glare at my mother through the walls. Come to think of it, I wasn't even sure if she was home. Nothing unusual about that. "I can guess."

My father put his big, hairy forearm up on the edge of the window and sized me up. He squinted through the glint of sunlight just over the rooftop of our house behind me. The sun had risen to midmorning by now, but a chill still clung to the air.

"How are my brother and sister?" I asked.

"They'll be thrilled to know I found you," he replied. "They're doing very well."

For a time there, it was almost pleasant, standing next to that idling car and speaking with a man my mother had spent the better part of my life demonizing. But as with anything in my life, the pleasantry would be short-lived. Of all people, my mother came striding out of the house. She had a way of walking noisily, her grumbling and heavy footsteps in the grass creating such a ruckus that she couldn't be ignored even if you wanted to. I turned away from her and rolled my eyes as she approached.

"Oh, you still look good," she yammered into the window.

The woman in my father's passenger seat assumed a sour expression.

I glanced at my mother with an eyebrow cocked. I had spent much of my life having no idea what would come out of her mouth next, and she never ceased to amaze.

"But I see you're still with that old battle-ax," she added, I guess referring to the woman in the driver's seat.

"Now you listen—" my father started to say, but he never got to finish the sentiment because my mother started kicking into her cat-in-heat behavior structure, going all crazy and saying crazier and nastier things with every frantic new breath. I tried holding her back, pulling her away from the car, but she dug her nails into my arm and lunged back at the window. She was so furious she might as well have been frothing at the mouth.

To my father's great credit, he didn't lose his cool. He stayed in the car, occasionally yelling something in defense of himself or his new wife, but never baiting my mother into a new round of insults. Unfortunately, she didn't need much baiting. The scene was getting hot, and I could feel the neighborhood's collective gaze wandering toward us, so I did the only thing I could think to do to throw water on the fire: I wrapped my arms around my mother's waist, threw her over my shoulder, and carried her fireman-style back to the house. She kicked and screamed the whole way, but I swear it was a matter of seconds after we got inside that she started to calm down. It was startling, and borderline comical, how docile she suddenly became.

"I can't believe you," I said.

"What?" she said defensively. "He started it."

I scoffed and turned back for the door. "Stay here," I called back over my shoulder. "I mean it."

My mother darted for the door just as it was closing between us. "He's *always* starting it," she barked loudly enough for my father to hear.

I made a motion for her to stay in the house, and so she slunk back into her lair. I found Big Joe shaking his head gravely as the woman beside him spoke harshly about my mother. When they noticed I had returned, they both softened into forced smiles.

"I'm sorry about that," Big Joe said.

"No," I said, shaking my head and looking back at the house. "I'm sorry." I shrugged. "You know how she is."

"Here," the woman said, reaching over my father to hand me a slip of paper.

"What's this?" I asked.

"It's our phone number," Big Joe said. "Give us a call, and we'll put you in touch with your brother and sister."

I nodded appreciatively as my father slid his hands to the steering wheel and gave it a quick smack. "Well, I guess we'd better be going."

"Thank you," I said.

He smiled with his eyes.

"No, I mean it. Thanks for stopping." Then, as he threw his car into drive, I remembered something. "How did you find me, anyway? I mean, after all these years—"

"You got pulled over," my father said. "I've been keeping an eye on police records for years in the hopes you'd turn up."

It hit me all at once. For more than a decade, the only thing keeping me from reuniting with the estranged half of my family was my lousy fake name. If I had thought to shirk trouble earlier in my life by giving my true name, we would have had this reunion years ago.

"No tickets in twelve years," my father said. "I guess you've been living on the straight and narrow."

I couldn't help the laugh. From the tension in my father's own laugh, I could tell he wasn't sure why I found his comment so funny. After a while, still chuckling, we said our goodbyes.

"I'll call you soon," I said.

"I hope you do, Joe," he said. "I hope you do."

And then they were gone.

A few days later, I left the house so I could call my father in peace. I dialed him from a pay phone in the parking lot where I usually sold drugs, my hands shaking from the nerves. It startled me how warm I felt when I heard his voice on the other end of the line. It wasn't because I took pleasure in reuniting with my father—I was still dealing with residual resentment dredged up by my mother, after all—but rather, it was because I knew this man represented my avenue back to David.

All my life, my mother had been telling me what a liar my father was, and yet he didn't even hesitate when I asked him for David's number. I thanked him genuinely, even though I was a little taken aback by how easy it was to get what I wanted. In that quick and light conversation, my father planted in me the first seed of doubt about what my mother had told me about him for all those years.

And then I called David. It had been years since I had heard my brother's voice, but it was still instantly familiar. The sound made my heart race and my eyes water. I don't remember much of what we said during the conversation, but I do remember crying heavily. Talking to him felt like bringing back to life a part of myself that I'd been hiding in the basement of my consciousness for years. It was like I'd packed away all the years of my life until the day I turned thirteen and my brother left—like all those deep wounds from a childhood wasted came rushing back, ready to be healed. More than that, hearing my brother's voice reminded me that the way I'd been living was a lie. My brother was my one true connection to the part of me that was real. I wasn't Joseph Carlucci. I was Joseph Adevai. And even though we didn't exchange much beyond details about where and when we would meet, talking to my brother made me see that for the first time in forever. Talking to my brother made me understand that, despite all the poor choices I'd made up to then, I could still *live* again.

By the time the appointed day of the meeting rolled around, I still hadn't managed to convince Karen and Stacey to join me in the reunion. I'm not sure why they were so standoffish about the matter. Maybe our mother had gotten to them. They were twenty-two and twenty years old at the time, but I guess still young enough to remain impressionable about our other family's quality of character. Even so, I wasn't about to leave without giving it at least one more chance.

Stacey was living with a girlfriend at the time, but I found Karen in the living room, watching TV, something she rarely did.

"Why don't you come with me?" I said to her for the fiftieth time that week.

Without looking away from her program, she made it clear that she was still refusing the offer. I couldn't believe how unreasonable she and Stacey were being about everything. David and Debbie had never done anything to either of them. In fact, for most of our fleeting time with our older siblings, they had done nothing but try to protect Karen and Stacey. But then I realized the problem. It was looming just behind me.

I turned to find my mother darkening the doorway, her eyes trained on the younger of her brood as if her mere gaze could keep them rooted there. Her glare always was rather supernatural, and this occasion was no different. Karen stayed put.

"I can't believe you," I said to my mother.

She kept staring at Karen. Even as I berated her for being too stubborn to let her own children reunite with a family that loved them, she didn't once look at me. After a time, I was struck with the notion that she had decided right then and there to disown me. She was ignoring me entirely, pretending as if I didn't exist. I don't know why it surprised me to see this. Her most recent threat was that if I decided to go see my older siblings, she would never speak to me again. My mother always was a professional when it came to following through on her threats. Even for as long as I had been trying to shut her out, to distance her from my life, and to minimize the effect she had on me, a part of me couldn't help but regret losing her. But then there was the other part of me that recognized immediately that this was the best possible thing that could happen to me. Being disowned by my mother was like winning the lottery of disownment.

I can't explain why I cried. I can't explain why the emotion so overwhelmed me that, even after walking three-quarters of a mile to a McDonald's parking lot in the pouring rain, I was still crying like a five-year-old with a skinned knee.

I was still sniveling when I made it to the lot—our designated meeting place—and it occurred to me that I might not recognize my brother after all these years.

But then I heard that familiar voice again. It was asking another man in the parking lot, "Are you Joe?"

I turned to see my brother just in time to watch him ask someone else if he was Joe. My heart stopped as he shrugged off the other man's reply and turned his gaze on me.

"Are you Joe?" he asked, looking like he knew the answer already.

"Yeah," I said, wiping away a tear with the meat of my palm. I was soaked from head to toe from the rain, but suddenly none of that mattered. "Yeah, I'm Joe."

My brother pulled me into an embrace, clapping one fist and then another into my back. Behind him, covering her smile with her hand as she huddled under an umbrella, was my sister Debbie. They looked so happy and so healthy and so welcome to my sore eyes. The three of us stood in that uninspiring place, slumping under the driving rain, but it was one of the greatest moments of my life.

In the moment, all I knew was joy. But as was the case with everything in my young life, I could sense that this joy would not be without its twin misery. Even as I accepted the lost love of my older brother and sister, I would be losing my mother and Karen and Stacey. I hadn't added new family to my life; I had merely traded the family I had always known for the family I didn't know.

"Should we go inside?" my brother asked.

As I wiped away a tear, I agreed. We walked side by side into the McDonald's, found a booth in the corner, and started the impossible task of catching up on all those lost years.

"You have no idea how relieved I was to hear you'd called David," Debbie said with a tearful smile.

"Yeah, it's been too long," I offered.

"No, you don't understand," she said. "We've been looking for you since the day you disappeared." Then she tumbled into a silent sob.

David offered a calm gaze. "We weren't sure what happened to you, Joe, so we feared the worst. You know how it was when I left you with her that day."

I nodded, remembering how close I'd come to letting my mother convince me to kill myself.

"Well, when you just disappeared completely," David added with a hesitant look at Debbie, "we feared that you'd all committed suicide or something terrible like that. We searched for clues. Hired a private detective. But it was like you just vanished into thin air."

"I don't know if you know how hard it was for us," Debbie said sadly. "You guys were younger. And since *she* was so absent, it was like we'd raised you ourselves. In some ways, losing the three of you was like losing our children."

"And we didn't know if you were alive, dead, out of the country, or what," David said.

"I'm so sorry," I said. "I didn't realize . . ." I didn't finish the thought because there was simply no way to express the totality of the things I didn't realize. I had been living in the dark all my life. In that corner booth at McDonald's, of all places, I saw the light for the first time.

We spent the rest of the conversation talking about the lost years. They discussed college and their marriages. I glossed over the troubling life I'd led. We talked about how we loved and missed each other, and about how it didn't matter what had happened in the past, because we were determined to make a better future together.

When it was over, I didn't know where to go. I wasn't comfortable asking my siblings for a place to crash, but I had a feeling I wouldn't be welcome back home. In the end, I kept the request to myself and slunk back to my former abode. There, I was glad to find everyone asleep. Even if my mother had truly disowned me, at least I would get one more peaceful night before the ugliness started anew.

The next morning, I woke early for work. I spent the day wrestling between the sorrow of being disowned and the hope for what the future might hold. It had been a long time since I had been hopeful, so I wasn't entirely sure how to deal with the sensation. That evening, I found the hope quashed by despair when I showed up to discover all my stuff sitting on the front porch. I wasn't sure what was more depressing: how devoted my mother was to cutting me out of her life or how very small my pile of stuff was. Everything I owned in the world could be stacked in one small corner of the porch in a lump no higher than my knee.

Then I remembered how I had nowhere to go. Briefly I pondered crashing with a friend, but I didn't know anyone who would be willing to take me in on such short notice while also making room for my stuff. So I called the only number I could think to call: my father's.

As I stood at that pay phone, listening to the ringing from the other end of the line, something remarkable occurred to me: I hadn't thought about cocaine in over twenty-four hours. I was so happy to have seen my brother and sister that the need never reached me. It's difficult to explain what it means to realize you don't need the substance you're addicted to, even if the lack of need only lasts a brief time. For me, it made me feel like I was getting my identity back.

For so long, I hadn't told anyone my real name. Not the girls I'd slept with or even my closest friends. Not once in a drug-induced stupor had I let down the false façade my mother had created for me.

But then, when my father answered the phone, it was like my true self had returned from the dark, dank place I had been keeping it locked away.

"Would it be okay if—" I started to say, but he cut me off before I had to ask.

"Of course you can stay with us," he said.

My father drove to Staten Island, where he picked me up at that same McDonald's parking lot and brought me back to his house in New Brunswick. He set me up in an extra bedroom and told me, with his wife, Pat, smiling warmly beside him, that I could stay with them until I got back on my feet. I had already taken a job at a bank in New York by then, so it felt like getting back on my feet was a real possibility.

"The first thing we're going to do," he told me, "is get your name back."

I wasn't sure what he meant at first, but over the weeks to come, I would stand in awe as my supposedly monstrous father would spend more than $2,500 on the process of getting my name legally changed back to Joseph Adevai. I had spent so long tarnishing my false name and living with my fake Social Security number that I could hardly believe it was even possible to return to my birth name. My father, in all his warmth and understanding, even agreed to let me keep "Carlucci" as my middle name after the switch.

There aren't words to explain how much I appreciated what my father and his wife did for me. Unfortunately, I still hadn't kicked my old habits, so it wasn't long before they figured out that I was a disaster.

God Sends Grapes

TAKING UP RESIDENCE with my father was a step in the right direction, but I still hadn't given up the cocaine. At first, he didn't know about my habit, but eventually he figured out that, on those frequent blowout weekends of mine, I was doing more than just drinking with friends. One excellent tip-off was that I would occasionally borrow his truck, drive to Staten Island, and then not return for days.

I don't know if it was a delayed "boys will be boys" kind of thing or if he was trying to help make up for lost time with me, but he kept the blinders on for a while longer than even the most patient among us probably would have. For instance, his answer to my frequent over-borrowing of his truck was to cosign a lease on a car for me. I'm not sure what he was thinking there, but I do know that, had our roles been reversed, there's no way in the world I would have helped me lease a car. I'd have just assumed it would wind up in a ditch or the impound lot or something. But that was my father: not at all the monster my mother had made him out to be for all those years. He was in many ways the first positive influence and role model I'd had since my brother left.

My reunion with my brother was every bit as uplifting for me at the time. I still had the lead weights around my neck—mostly the drugs, but also the women that weren't exactly helping to steer me toward the straight and narrow—but my brother kept a level head and an even keel with me. I've often thought that bringing me into his life probably felt a little like adopting an abused dog. There's love and affection in there somewhere; you just have to wait for all the old, skittish habits to fade away.

As it happened, I was with one of those less-than-helpful girlfriends at the time I first met my brother and his wife for dinner. The four of us set up in a booth at Beefsteak Charlie's, a place I still mourn for its spectacular but wildly shortsighted business model of all-you-can-eat salad bar and all-you-can-drink beer, wine, and sangria. I remember the conversation was awkward at first. There was my brother in this nice, loving relationship with a wife that supported and cared for him, and there I was with a girl whose name I sometimes forgot while riding the downward crest of a cocaine high. My brother was wearing the white coat of an atomic scientist researching particle smashing at Cornell. I was going to Studio 54 every Saturday and waking up in people's houses with guns to my head or girls I didn't recognize lying beside me. My brother and I had almost nothing in common and no shared history to carry us through. So I did what anyone would do: I focused on the food and booze.

It took me a while to notice that my brother and his wife weren't drinking. In fact, it was my girlfriend that pointed it out.

"Oh. Right," my brother said, seeming kind of nervous about the subject.

"Yeah, what happened, man?" I asked. "You pregnant or something." I was chock-full of tact in those days.

My brother and his wife smiled politely. "No," he said. "I'm Christian now."

I remember setting my fork down and looking at him funny. Coming up together, our house hadn't been the most formative in the best of times, but to think that one of my siblings was Christian just boggled my mind. The concept was so foreign that he might as well have said he had become a camel.

"How?" is what I managed to ask through my dumb, open-mouthed surprise.

With their hands laced over each other, my brother and his wife told the story in a way that suggested this wasn't their first time telling it.

"When we first met," my brother said, "I just couldn't get her out of my head."

His wife rolled her eyes playfully. "He was like a moth to light."

My smile was genuine. I don't think my girlfriend's was.

"She told me she wouldn't go out with a non-Christian," my brother explained.

"So he said to me that it didn't make sense to believe in God," she said.

"But I wanted to be with her." My brother paused for a moment as if pondering all the grace and good fortune he had found in God's favor. "So we made a bet of sorts."

They looked at each other and giggled.

"I said that I was going to prove her wrong," he explained. "I told her that if I could prove that God didn't exist, she would have to go out with me."

"But he couldn't!" his wife interrupted.

My girlfriend grumbled under her breath and got up to use the salad bar for the third time. It wasn't with a wistful look that I watched her leave.

"You're always breaking in at the best parts," my brother said to his wife in a gentle, ribbing sort of way. They shared a contented smile before he continued. "So, yeah, I spent two years trying to prove that God didn't exist and Christianity was nonsense. I turned to every piece of scientific evidence I could think of, and even expanded into research on subjects like archeology, astrophysics, and philosophy. None of them made the point for me."

"But . . . ," I said, my depth of surprise causing me to trail off. "But you're a *scientist*."

He shrugged.

"Aren't you supposed to believe in science?"

"Oh, I do believe in science." He leaned forward to set his elbow on the table and his chin in his hand, giving me that practiced psychiatrist's sort of stare—the one that's neither aloof nor condescending, the one that suggests a casual sort of intensity on the part of the speaker. "When I was trying to prove God doesn't exist, I found plenty of evidence that science provides tremendous insight. Science was my religion, and in some ways, it still is. I don't see science and religion as opposing viewpoints anymore. They intertwine, each of them providing us a glimpse of our purpose in this life."

Not knowing how to respond, I shook my head. Then I took a long, healthy sip of my wine. It was around that time that my girlfriend returned. She slid truculently into the booth as if sending a message that she was starting to feel like there were many places in the world she would rather be than here. I had to agree with her: There were many places in the world I would rather she have been than here.

"The bottom line is that I couldn't prove that God didn't exist," my brother said. He wore this expression that I didn't recognize back then. In the years to come, I would learn that it is the kind of expression that you only find in people who carry the light of God and all the contentment and joyful assuredness that comes with it. "So I did the next best thing. I started researching Christianity." He and his wife shared a long, meaningful gaze. "When I came back to her, it was as a Christian. She was right, I told her."

"And the rest is history," she finished for him.

I could actually feel my girlfriend roll her eyes. When our main courses arrived, she dug in ravenously. Normally I'd have joined her in the display, but I was so entranced by what my brother had just told me that I didn't do much more than pick at my food.

When it was over and we were preparing to say our goodbyes, he slid a book across the table to me. "This is for you," he said.

It was a Bible. When I picked it up, my girlfriend gave me this strange look like she thought maybe touching it was going to give me a rash.

"You don't have to read it if you don't want to," my brother added. "I just thought you'd like to have it."

I thanked him for it—and at the time, I meant my thanks genuinely—but after we parted and I got back out to the parking lot and my newly leased and still somehow accident-free car, it didn't take me long to return to myself. My girlfriend and I jabbered about the incident for a while, but the consensus quickly became that we thought my brother was crazy for giving me a Bible. Back then, I was still more likely to do lines *off* that Bible than read lines out of it.

But something about that conversation did stick with me. It haunted me for quite a while, in fact. It wasn't the notion that God had changed my brother for the better—although I have to believe that this revelation remained in the back of my mind, no matter how hard I tried to fight it. Rather, it was the positive relationship he had with his wife that opened my eyes to how I was living. After that initial conversation and the gift of the Bible, I was convinced that it wasn't God I needed if I wanted to pull myself out of the gutter; it was the love of a good woman. As we drove back toward my girlfriend's apartment and all the drugs and debauchery I knew awaited us there, I had a keen sense that this was not the woman to play my rescuer.

As I meandered back toward at least a somewhat respectable life, I somehow managed to land a job as a clerk on the trading floor at the New York Futures Exchange. If not for my fortuitous name change, I'm sure they'd have never let a guy with my criminal history anywhere near the building, much less on the floor. I was still a drug abuser and serial pseudo-monogamist, but I supposed I couldn't have been the only one. It was the '80s, and cocaine was the lifeblood of many in the industry. Anyway, they paid me $300 a week for the gig, which was an unimaginable sum of money for me back then, so I didn't complain and I always showed up for work on time.

So there I was, living in a stable home, with a good job, and riding the commuter train from New Brunswick into Manhattan every morning. I was a nearly respectable contributor to the greater good of society. At least that's what I looked like on the outside. On the inside, my mind still roiled with doubt and addiction and more doubt. I drifted through each day with this weird combination of confidence in my abilities to do this job and confidence in the notion that eventually I was going to screw up somehow. I was trying to pull myself out of the churning waters of failure, and I had proven a reasonably strong swimmer. But failure is a raging, storm-rocked, *angry* ocean. What I needed was a lifeline.

My lifeline carried a briefcase and wore a long, gray raincoat. She was beautiful—stunning, really—but she looked tired in that way people look when they're dragging themselves to a job they hate. Maybe it was just the briefcase and the clear effort she had made to look good, but I got the sense that she was far too sophisticated to be interested in one of those trademark monosyllabic advances that had gotten me in the good graces of a woman or two at Studio 54.

Still, I was nothing if not a determined young man. I didn't approach her that day, but I did sear her image into my memory, and I did say something to myself that surprised even me.

"I'm gonna marry that girl," I said under my breath.

As I watched her board a different car, I couldn't help but wonder if I'd gone crazy. I'd only seen this woman for a few seconds, and the ride would pass without me saying a word to her, but something told me this was the girl I would marry.

I guess it was partly in an effort to reaffirm my beliefs, but that night at dinner with my father and stepmother, I let them know the big news.

"I saw the girl I'm gonna marry today," I said.

Both of them stopped chewing and looked at me wide-eyed. I think maybe they misunderstood me at first and were concerned that I'd decided to marry one of the less reputable young women I was dating at the time.

"You *saw* this girl?" my stepmother asked.

"That's right," I said. I picked up my wine as if to toast the room, but then just set it back down.

"What's her name?" my father asked.

"Oh, I don't know." I shrugged. "I just saw her is all."

"You mean you didn't even *talk* to her?"

"Didn't get a chance. I was already on the train when I saw her on the platform. She got on a different car and must have gotten off at a different stop."

My father and stepmother shared a look like they thought maybe I was high. I wasn't, though. I didn't get high at all that day. I guess I was just buzzing from seeing my future wife.

Then my father started laughing and clapped me once on the shoulder. "Well, it sounds good, kid," he said. "But maybe you should try talking to her next time."

The next time wouldn't come for another few months. On that occasion, I boarded the train and decided that I would walk up and down through the cars until I found an acceptable seat. By "acceptable seat," I mean a seat beside a pretty woman. I must have been going through a dry spell, because I was essentially returning to an old well. I had met a few girls on the train and had gone out with them. I always thought it was easier talking to the Jersey girls on the train than the New York chicks at the clubs. But I was coming off a long stretch of not exactly needing easier talking.

I think I'd made it through three cars, striking out in every one, before I saw her. There was no seat beside her, but I knew I had to stop here and at least try to get her attention. Unfortunately, she was lying with her head back, sleeping.

There she is, I thought. *The One.*

Not knowing what to do—I mean, I didn't want to wake her up for fear that it might annoy her—I just kept walking. I wanted to grab the nearest seat and just spend the rest of the ride stealing looks at her, but then, I also didn't want to be a creep. So I enjoyed one last quick glance and passed her by. She really was a vision. I still didn't know anything about her, but being near her, even if only for a moment, even if we couldn't speak, reinforced my feeling that I was meant to be with this woman. I found a seat in the next car, this one beside an old man, all my desire for conquest having left me at the sight of the woman I would come to love.

It was a long three months of pining before I saw her again. This time, she saw me first. I was walking up the steps to the train when something compelled me to look back. There she was, and she was staring at me—I mean *really* giving me the eye. At first, I thought maybe she was just sort of staring in my direction, but after I reached the top of the steps and looked back again, it was clear she only had eyes for me. To see such desire written on the face of the woman I had wanted for so long sent a jolt through me that I can't properly explain.

I reacted like a schoolboy: I bolted and found a lonely seat on the train.

Now the seats on the Jersey Transit are interesting because some of them face each other. I'd never had much use for that feature before. In fact, most of the time when I had to sit across from someone, I found it really uncomfortable. We'd have to pass all the time either making small talk or avoiding each other's gazes so we didn't have to make small talk. But on this occasion, I couldn't have been happier to choose the seat I chose.

The woman found me. She sought me out. I could hardly believe it, but here she was, short of breath as if she'd had to trot to keep up with me, taking a seat right across from me. I was shocked and a little scared. Suave as I always fancied myself to be, I found it difficult to speak.

Wait a minute, I thought. *Do I really want to get married right now?*

That's how sure I was that this woman was the one. I thought that just sitting and speaking with her would lead to immediate marriage, and considering the state I was in at the time, that sounded like a lousy idea, if not just terrible timing.

When finally I allowed myself to look back at her, the first thing I noticed was that she had this scratch on the side of her face. She was pretty, but the sight of the scratch was unsettling enough to make me rethink my conviction, if only for a moment. She wasn't the type I was used to dating. My fare fell more into the big-haired, spastic-'80s kinds of girls, and the One looked more like a buttoned-down career girl. She hadn't painted her makeup on in garish fashion, as I was used to. She hadn't teased her hair into a caricature of a Brillo pad, as I was used to. She was showing far less skin than I was used to. She looked startlingly pretty, but in a way that was far more understated than I had come to expect in the women with whom I spent time.

"Hi," she said.

I feigned confusion. "Do I know you from somewhere?" Then I thought, *Did I really just say that? Is that out of a movie or something? I can't even believe how cheesy that sounded.*

Whatever flaws to be found in my reply, they didn't seem to faze her. She was smart and funny, and we enjoyed a quick and easy rapport. Her name was Alicia. She couldn't have been more charismatic, and really, it was that charisma that rendered me into a tactless oaf.

"So what's with the scratch on your head?" I asked her.

She blushed a little and turned her face slightly as if to hide it. "Is it that noticeable?"

I shrugged. "Yeah. I guess." I forced a laugh in an effort to soften the blow.

"It's from my cat."

"So you're a cat lady, huh?"

Her lips curled at the corners. "What's a cat lady?"

"You know," I said. "Those ladies that live with a bunch of cats."

She scrunched her face into mock outrage. "I'm not a spin-ster, if that's what you mean."

"But you *are* single," I said. It wasn't a question. I just knew and didn't care to hide it.

"I am."

"And you have cats."

"*A* cat," she corrected.

"Well, there you have it," I said, turning up my palms. "Cat lady."

Her warm smile just about floored me. I couldn't believe how comfortable it made me feel, how at peace and how right with the world I was when I saw it. But the moment was fleeting, because the train would be stopping soon and I didn't yet know what to do about this obvious connection we had. I didn't want to blow my opportunity with the girl I would marry, but at the same time, I didn't want to be overly aggressive either. Maybe I could just suggest that we meet on the train again sometime. That would be less forward than asking for her number.

"Can I have your number?" I heard myself saying. My mind immediately objected to the tack I had taken, but I couldn't stop myself from adding, "Maybe we can go out to dinner sometime."

My heart raced as she pulled out a pen and a scrap of paper from her briefcase and started writing her number. The train chose that moment to stop, and so we parted all giddy and pretending not to be giddy. There are few feelings like it in the world, that fresh, electric feeling derived from that combination of raw attraction, flattery, and excitement about the possibilities the future holds.

Keeping to male protocol, I waited a day to call her. We hit it off, completely and immediately. Plans were made to meet up soon. I very much looked forward to seeing how we would fare at dinner.

Apparently Alicia couldn't wait, because she decided to pay me a visit at work on the day before our first date.

I'd already drudged most of a long day answering phones from the trading floor. I'd spent many hours frantically taking orders and signaling them into the pit. That's part of why I was so beside myself when someone approached me and said there was a young lady in to see me. The other part of why is that people didn't usually just *walk* onto the trading floor. The scene was made stranger still by the fact that everyone sort of stopped what they were doing the moment they saw her. There were only a few women who worked in the building, so when a pretty woman showed up, everything came to a grinding halt so the men could get in a good gawk.

Alicia was all dressed up for work, briefcase in hand and her hair and makeup just so. In her other hand, she carried a paper bag whose purpose I couldn't imagine. What I could imagine were the furrowed brows of the traders that watched her walking past. It seemed everyone was as confused as I was about the pretty lady and the bag she carried.

"Hey," she said when she reached my desk. She was all smiles. "I was in the neighborhood, so I thought I'd stop by. Here . . ." She held out the bag for me. "I got this for you."

I was puzzled as I took the gift and opened it. It was a bag of grapes. Over her shoulder, I could see many of the traders and other clerks chuckling. It was completely embarrassing. Still, I liked her. A great deal. I still believed I would marry her. In that moment, holding those grapes, I decided that I was going to get straight. I hadn't yet given up drugs, or even looking around at other women, but right then and there, I decided that I was done. Since the day I started living with my father, I had hoped for some sort of deliverance from my addictions to drugs and shady behavior. God had granted that deliverance in the form of Alicia.

And Alicia had brought me grapes.

こ

My in-the-moment vow to give up drugs turned out to be just that: in-the-moment. Even though my dates with Alicia were going well and we were connecting on a level I had never experienced before, I still had a long way to go in my quest to become a decent human being. I was still living with my father, still getting high, and still staying out all weekend every weekend. The sleep deprivation from my constant highs would cause me to do classy things like falling asleep on trains and getting stuck at the end of the line. Once I ended up in Trenton and had to spend the night sleeping on a park bench.

It was around that time that it started to bother my father. I'd just come back from a three-day bender. I hadn't slept in two nights. I staggered in all bleary-eyed and sallow to find my father and his wife sitting at the table with that histrionic look of deep concern.

"Sit down, son," my father said.

I hesitated. Even strung out, I wasn't so far gone that I couldn't sense what was about to happen.

"C'mon, Joe," he said. "Please."

Slowly I took a seat across from them. My stepmother offered me coffee, which I declined. There's a weird thing that happens when you push your body to the brink like that: for a startlingly long time, it stops wanting anything. Then, all at once—zing!—you're *burning* to return to all those biological functions you've been ignoring for days and days.

"We can't have this," my father said. "If you spend another weekend away—if you do this one more time—you're out."

My first instinct was to get defensive and angry, but I quickly let it calm. I could see that they cared about me. This wasn't some unreasonable expectation laid on me by a man who only recently became my father again. This was a loving parent acting out of genuine concern. So I sat there in my half-zombified state, and I made the solemn vow never to do it again.

Two weeks later I did it again.

They threw me out.

It was the best thing they ever could have done for me.

Since I was still a bonehead, I made the brilliant choice to move to Staten Island, where many of my negative influences and opportunities for poor choices still resided. My cushy paychecks helped me land an apartment on my own dime, and quickly the place became Cocaine Highway. I'd lowered my levels of consumption—I owed that much to my job and Alicia—but my friends still partied like the end was nigh.

My father and brother must have been working at least slightly in concert, because around that same time of the great kick-out, David started coming around more often and talking to me about God.

My relationship with Alicia was developing nicely, but the drugs kept digging new holes in my heart. I figured that maybe God could help me fill it, so I really was trying to get into it. The problem was that I was still so cynical and self-righteous. I wasn't yet ready to let go and allow God to steer me back toward the path. David responded by sliding me a copy of a novel called *Quo Vadis*. The book is about a Roman patrician and soldier named Marcus Vinicius who falls for a Christian girl named Lygia. This was before the time of the Roman conversion to Christianity, so the underlying themes deal mostly with Vinicius's struggle to reconcile being a soldier dedicated to Rome and a man dedicated to Jesus.

The book spoke to me on a profound level because, even though Alicia wasn't a Christian at the time, I identified her with Lygia. She was similarly steadfast in her beliefs, and yet kind, caring, and understanding to me in exactly the same way as Lygia was with Vinicius. We would argue about various social and spiritual issues, only to reconcile shortly after. Sometimes I would show up on her doorstep, completely wasted, and she would take me in and do whatever it took to return me to sobriety. Like Lygia to Vinicius, Alicia represented the good, the hope, and the inspiration in my life.

Then around Christmas of 1986, she wanted me to come with her to meet her family for the first time. Given the house I grew up in, holidays were never much my thing. By then, I had already started viewing them solely as opportunities to get crazy. That's the thing about occasions where traditional families gather together: Those without traditional families—particularly those with a bent for self-destruction—tend to want to ramp up their efforts at achieving chemical anarchy. So I had plans.

Alicia didn't push me at first, but then a few days before the holiday, she put her foot down. "Look," she said. "If you don't come with me to meet my parents, we're done."

My first instinct was to feel relieved. I can't properly explain it, but I think it had something to do with the sheer weight of my love for her. I had never felt so close or so completely in need of someone before. Almost from the start, it was as if I could see no way to quit this woman. That stood in stark contrast to my usual relationships, where I could look for and find a way out immediately. So here was Alicia offering me a way to turn my back on the best thing that ever happened to me. And there I was looking forward to more opportunities to self-destruct.

It took me longer than it should have to decide what I was going to do. Ultimately it was the lessons of Marcus Vinicius that compelled me to make the trip. As I sat slumped at my desk at work—that particular trading day having drained me to the core—I dialed her number and let her know I'd be along for the ride. She sounded relieved that I had made the right decision.

When we arrived at Alicia's house, I met her brother Alan and her sister Alana first. They seemed like good people—kind and welcoming from the moment we said hello. But then I met Alicia's stepfather and his daughters from his first marriage. I had pieced together that the stepfather had been physically abusive to Alan and sexually abusive to Alicia and Alana. It reminded me so much of my mother's relationships that I cringed just to be near him. His presence hung a pall over the whole affair.

His daughters lived in Georgia and had made the trip up for the holiday. Being Southern belles, and born-again Christians besides, they were a charming pair. One of them latched onto the notion that I was a recently converted Christian, so she started talking to me about "Jeeesus" in her adorable Southern twang. I poured myself into the conversation because the subject interested me, but more so because it seemed to me that Jesus was suddenly approaching me from all angles of my life. Everywhere I turned, I was met with messages of Jesus. I figured it had to mean something, so even though Alicia had asked me not to talk religion at this gathering, I wound up talking religion almost the whole time. It made the visit more enjoyable than I'd thought it would be, but the ride home with Alicia was less than pleasant. We fought about how I'd brought up Jesus again. I found myself hoping that my girlfriend would experience the light of God soon.

It was maybe three weeks later when a cocaine binge led me to my first genuine experience with God. I hadn't slept for three days and had missed a few days of work. It was eleven o'clock in the evening when I got back to my apartment in Staten Island. I didn't want to call Alicia because I was sick of driving to New Brunswick to have her nurse me back to health. Since there was no one else I could call, depression began to sink in.

Some people find God out of curiosity. Some people find God naturally over the course of their lives. Some people are born into their beliefs. For me, I found God because I was as depressed as I can ever remember being.

"God," I said—and I was actually on my knees praying. It was an awkward position for me, so I'm sure I looked every bit as uncomfortable as I felt. "God, if you're really there, you know I can't do this anymore. Every time I use, I just want to die." When I heard no immediate reply, I started to panic. I leapt to my feet and started pacing around my apartment like a caged animal. "I can't do this anymore," I kept saying. "I can't do this anymore." Like some bad cartoon, I was actually pulling at my hair as I endured my breakdown.

I felt like I was in a box I couldn't escape. I had a sense that, no matter what I did or who I turned to, I would always wake up with those same feelings. There was no way out. Nothing could cure the holes I had made in my own heart—not drugs, not money, not women, not more drugs, not more women, not drugs and drugs and drugs. No matter what I did, I would fail. I was certain of it. I would lose my job on the back of some binge. I would blow it with Alicia on mistakes made while high. I loved my job and was crazy about Alicia. I could sense that they were my deliverance. But at the same time, I knew I didn't deserve them.

Not even God wants to talk to me, I thought, and that was enough to make me spiral into depths I couldn't possibly describe and knew that I would never escape.

Then it hit me: There was one outlet left to me that would be much easier than repairing my relationships, quitting the drugs, and learning to accept God's guidance. There was still that one escape about which my mother had taught me.

All it took was a knife. Or some pills. All it took was an ender. Then all the pain would lift. Then I would be in that peaceful place she once promised me. There would be no suffering there. No regret or remorse. There would only be nothing.

The nothing was so desirable that it filled my head to where I thought my skull would burst. I tumbled into my secondhand sofa and pressed my head in my hands. I wanted to scream and explode and dissipate into the nothing. I wanted nothing more than to be nothing more. My own scream echoed in my head, reverberating and redoubling until it was so loud it was all I could hear or see or feel.

And then the strangest thing happened. I pulled my hands back and opened my eyes, and there, right in front of me on the table, was that little black Bible my brother had given me. I couldn't imagine what had compelled me to leave it out in the open like that. I never had any intention of reading it. But right then, at 2:00 a.m. on one of the most ragged nights of my life, it seemed to call to me.

I picked it up.

On the inside cover, I saw that my brother had written me a note: *To Joe. Read the book of John first. From your brother, David Dean.*

So I started reading the Gospel of John. After two chapters, I felt like I should keep reading. By chapter three, I started to piece together that the red lettering in this NIV version of the Bible indicated that Jesus was talking. When I started to focus on those words, I felt like there was absolute truth in everything he said. I didn't really understand the depth of this truth until I reached John 3:17, which reads, *For God did not send His Son into the world to condemn the world, but that the world through Him might be saved.*

It was then that I woke up.

At John 3:19-20, I read, *This is the condemnation, that the light is come into the world, and men loved darkness rather than light, because their deeds were evil. For everyone practicing evil hates the light and does not come to the light, lest his deeds should be exposed.*

"Oh my God!" I said.

The letters were leaping off the page at me. It was almost like a high. The messages I was reading grabbed me and held me. God had my attention. My heart raced with every new passage and every new realization that Jesus knew *everything about me.*

The effect was dual. On the one hand, I was uplifted. On the other, I felt ashamed of the life I had led to that point. I wanted to keep it all in the dark, wanted to erase it from memory and record and the lives of everyone I knew.

I had lived my whole life in the dark. From the time I was fourteen, I began hating my life, doing drugs, and avoiding sleep and constructive relationships and reality in general. It was a darkness I embraced, for it shielded the true me from the people I knew.

But the words of Jesus shined a light on me. I don't know if I was born again right there, but I do know that, while I was reading, something miraculous happened. Something inside me changed.

The next day, I called David. "This guy knows everything about me," I explained.

"I had a feeling that Bible might surprise you," he said with a warm chuckle. "Did you read John?"

"Front to back," I said, and then I started rambling excitedly about all the lessons I had learned. My brother encouraged and congratulated me all the while.

When we prepared to end the conversation, I knew I had to find the words to thank him, but there was nothing I could say that could come close to the gratitude I knew. But as I stammered through an attempt at thanks, he stopped me.

"You don't have to thank me, Joe," he said. "You found Jesus all on your own, and it's Him you should be thanking. I just passed you the message."

Around the same time that I was awakening to the messages of Jesus, Alicia was wavering in her commitment to our relationship. I can't blame her. She had stuck by me for so many long nights and weekends of drug abuse and other unsavory behavior. When she left me for someone else, it throttled me, but still I understood it. I even tried to go along with it by taking a girl I'd met out for some dinner, but we didn't get five minutes into the date before I realized that it wasn't going anywhere—and that nothing would go anywhere, save for with Alicia.

That night, I prayed that Alicia might one day find her way to Jesus too. Not long after, I picked up the phone to the sound of this dulcet, utterly contented voice. The sound of it was so different that I didn't recognize it as Alicia at first.

"What's going on with you?" I asked. "You sound different."

"I've been born again, Joe," she said.

An unparalleled warmth filled me from within. "I've been praying for you," I said, tears lining my eyes.

The more she spoke, the harder I cried. I couldn't believe the transformation in this woman who had claimed to be done with me only a few days prior. Now she was telling me that she had given her heart to God. To this day, I have never seen anything quite like what happened with my wife.

Naturally, I wanted to see her, but even with all the progress I was making on my path back to God, I still hadn't managed to kick the cocaine. The next time we met, I was high. I expected that to be the end, but she was unimaginably kind to me. I knew her friends were telling her to let me go, but every time I showed up stoned, she would nurse me back to sobriety.

Every time I went back to cocaine, I got more desperate. There came a point when I was finding myself partying all night, then spending six or seven hours in the car the next morning, just driving around in search of someone who might take me in instead of Alicia. I just didn't want her to see me like that anymore, and yet I couldn't stop *making myself* like that. Every time, I would run out of options—I had burned every bridge and soured every relationship by then—and wind up at her house. Every time, she would accept me with open arms.

On one such day, it had to be midafternoon by the time I knocked on her door. I'm sure I smelled like a barroom floor and looked like a sewer rat. It didn't matter to her. It never mattered. She helped me stagger to her sofa and crash. There I lay for a while as she made some tea and gathered up some expired aspirin. Before she returned, I felt the weight of my addiction crash down on me. I was lying there with my face buried in a couch cushion, praying to God to just help me find some relief, and I saw—not for the first time, but certainly in the most profound of ways—the contrast in what I was doing. I was coming down from a bender and asking God to help me stop going on these benders. The awful truth of it was like a punch in the back of the head.

Softly at first, but then so violently I could hardly breathe, I began to cry into that cushion.

It wasn't long before I felt Alicia's gentle touch on my back. She sat beside me and comforted me until I calmed down enough to stop sobbing. I waited for her to tell me that it would be all right, like she always did, but instead, she said something completely unexpected.

"You've got to stop this."

All at once, my tears returned. I bellowed into the couch for another minute or so before I pulled myself together enough to sit up and face her. I could see that she meant what she had said. She was patient and kind, but in her expression I could read that even patience and kindness has its limits. She was saved, and I was claiming to be saved but behaving as if I still lived in the darkness. I didn't know what to do or say. I wanted to run and hide in a small, dark hole. But something kept me rooted there. Something bigger than myself and bigger even than our relationship.

"I need you to pray for me," I said.

She nodded her solemn vow to do just that. As a woman born again, she promised that she would.

"But you're not going to do it anymore," she said. It wasn't a question. She was telling me how it would be. "I'm not going to see the man that showed up at my door today anymore. Do you understand?"

I nodded, that pain of sorrow forming in my throat once more.

"Good," she said. And then her expression softened. "When do you want to get married? In the spring or the fall?"

At that point, I was still groggy. I hadn't slept for days, and now I was vowing never to do drugs again and to accept her love and God's guidance and I had no idea what she was talking about when she asked me when we would get married.

"I'm sorry, what?" I said.

"Spring or fall?" she repeated. "What sounds best to you?"

My mind raced. I was so out of it that it took me several seconds just to remember the month and year. It was February of 1987. That much I knew. And after some careful math, I figured out that the spring was a scant two months away. So I took the only option that made sense to me at the time.

"The fall sounds great," I said.

And that was it. We were getting married in the fall. I was never going to do drugs again and we were both born again and we were getting married in the fall and I was never going to do drugs again.

"I'm never going to do drugs again," I said, and we embraced. "I'm never going to do drugs again."

CHAPTER SIX

The Pieces

THE DAY I first did drugs again was shortly after I bought Alicia her diamond. I picked up the stone from my father's friend at a cost of $1,000. Then I found a gold wedding band, and after some dealmaking, got somebody to slap the two together. It was at the engagement party—or more directly, it was *after* the engagement party—when I started steering myself back toward that cliff.

Poor Alan. Alan was Alicia's brother. He and I hit it off quickly, and that's why I call him "Poor Alan." Barring Alicia, who had an iron will, anyone who hit it off with me in those days was as likely to wake up in a ditch with a searing hangover as they were their own bed. It didn't help the cause that all my friends from Staten Island came for the party. Alicia's mother—who was right never to fully trust or like me—kept her eyes wide and her head on a swivel whenever my buddies and me came near anything she valued. Our presence didn't seem to bother Alan, so I figured I'd ask if he wanted to stick with us for a while. I thought of it as family bonding, I suppose.

"Hey, you want to go out after this?" I asked him.

He looked just like an excited kid from a '50s sitcom. He might as well have said, "Boy, do I!" in reply.

So when the party was over, I took him to Staten Island and got us some cocaine. When we had honked it all, we went to Brooklyn to a bodega I knew and scored some more.

"Listen," I told Alan as we approached the store, "these guys are serious dealers. Let me do the talking."

I don't know if it was the high he was bouncing on or his naiveté, but Alan laughed as if I was putting him on.

"No, I mean it," I insisted. "You say the wrong thing here, you're liable to get shot."

He went white as a sheet, and clammed up after that. I had him full of quite a lot of cocaine, but no amount of blow can make a novice abuser confident in the face of a loaded firearm.

In the store, he did as I told him, I said all the right things, and we escaped with another reasonable stash. The store owners were clever. They never handed over the product directly. In exchange for my cash, they slid a milk carton back at me. Outside, I saw that they had taped the drugs to the bottom of the carton. As I unstrapped enough snow for a two-day bender, I remember taking the briefest moment of pause as we exited the place. Just for a second—little more than half a heartbeat—I thought maybe I should take Alan home instead of out to the clubs. I was concerned that, in the first night of knowing him, I was going to either get him shot, or worse, corrupt him forever.

For the next few days, we crashed in a penthouse belonging to the sister of a friend named Joanie, a woman who would later come to Jesus. It was just a typical weekend for me, but to Alan, it was the most amazing thing he had ever experienced. I knew this because he kept telling me about how amazing it all was.

At some point, though—I think it was about the morning of the second day—Alan started telling me we should probably go home.

"Are you kidding?" I said, my vision blurry and my mind wild. "If I take you home now, Alicia's gonna kill me."

The longer we stayed and partied and the more frequently Alan asked to be taken home, the more terrified I became that I had screwed up completely this time.

"Look, why don't you take a taxi?" I said right around dusk on that second day. "I'll call for it and give the guy some cash to get you home."

I'm not sure whether Alan was naturally afraid to go off on his own in the big city or if it was just the drugs, but the idea seemed to frighten him. My solution to the problem, and to any problem really, was more cocaine. In that white, intoxicating snow, I tried to bury my regret at doing this to Alicia and her brother.

It was a Thursday when we started the party. I brought Alan back on Saturday afternoon. Naturally, our welcoming committee wasn't the cheeriest. As we approached a clearly livid Alicia and her mother, I elbowed Alan, trying to get him to buck up, but he was a walking zombie. He had never even been *near* so many drugs, let alone ingested them, so he was more than a little out of it.

"Alicia, please," I said, my voice quavering already. "I'm sorry. I know what I did was wrong, I just couldn't—"

"We're going to church tomorrow," Alicia snapped. She snatched her brother by the collar, and although he was much larger than her, it looked to me like she could have taken him down if she wanted. "You're *both* going to church tomorrow!"

The next morning, Alan and I were like two children avoiding the early rise and the need for fine clothes. We took a bitter breakfast and followed Alicia—who played the role of mother well, I noticed—out to the car and on to a small church on Livingston Avenue in New Brunswick.

As foggy as my week had been, I had no idea what was in store for me that day. Alicia sat between me and her brother during the service. I was so weak and hungover that it was all I could do to keep from swaying in the pew. I'm sure Alan was feeling the same way. My mind was so gone that I understood very little of what the little white-haired preacher was saying, but I did perk up when he started talking about Jesus dying for my sins.

"Jesus died on the cross so that you could be saved," the preacher said. "This means that, if you receive him into your heart today, you can have eternal life. I ask that you bow your heads and pray with me for this blessing."

I bowed my head, a new sort of reverence falling over me.

"Is there anyone among us who would like to receive Jesus today?" the preacher asked.

I shook my head as if clearing it of the fog.

He asked again.

In that moment, I felt a strange heat rise in my chest. I stopped concentrating on my hangover and how I had no desire to be here and suddenly felt utterly compelled to raise my hand. I had known for years that I had to repair my ways. This was just the first moment when I realized *how*.

There my future wife sat beside me. She had already become everything I wanted to become. And she had done so through the power of Jesus. This was my deliverance, I understood.

So I raised my hand.

ॐ

After that, it was almost like I was addicted to getting saved. Alicia and I started visiting churches, looking for a place to call our spiritual home, and at every stop, I would get saved again. Despite our new and purer life, I had nowhere else to go, so I lived with Alicia. I felt guilty about our living together without technically being married yet. When I told her about it, she admitted to feeling the same way, so we agreed that we would share a roof, but we wouldn't sleep in the same bed until we got married. We lived like that for six months.

I can't believe I'm doing this, I would think, and I would think that at least once a day. But then that thought began to fade the more I realized that my love for her was something more than anything I had thought possible. I desired her, but not in the way I did when I pursued girls just for sex. I desired her sexually, of course, but it was more than that. She represented everything that was good about my life. She represented my deliverance from evil.

We were married on November 14, 1987. The weather was perfect, warm and clear. It was a typical Staten Island wedding, which is to say that it was sprawling with groomsmen and bridesmaids, twelve a side. Alicia was gorgeous in her white dress. The moment I saw her walking down the aisle, I knew for sure that we were meant to be together forever. When it was over, we took our big bag of envelopes and went off to the Dominican Republic for a week-long honeymoon that wound up stretching to two weeks. We quickly learned that marriage was a gas.

Not long after we returned home, we started attending services at the Church of Christ in New York, which set up shop at the Beacon Theater. It was an absolutely enormous church, with some two thousand attendees at every service, an a cappella worship, and a baptism for dozens of people every week. Being still somewhat new to churchgoing, I was blown away by the sheer spectacle of it all. The teaching was good, of course, but it was mostly the excitement of the young people in attendance that made my heart churn. Because the church was so large, it would split into "zones," or smaller groups of people headed up by appointed leaders. Ted and Cathy, friends with someone Alicia knew in college, became our leaders. It had nothing to do with Ted and Cathy themselves, but it was in this group that I first started getting some pushback about the pieces of my life I had yet to pick up.

"So you mean to tell me that you're still doing cocaine?" someone asked me. She was incredulous, and I'll leave her nameless for obvious reasons. Her husband shared in her indignation, and together they formed a front against me.

"I'm still trying to—"

"You've got to be kidding me." He cut me off.

Alicia and I exchanged a glance of bewilderment. I had been under the impression that church services and the zones they spawned would be safe, accepting places, no matter what. But here I found myself pressured from all sides for details about the shadier parts of my life. I wanted to talk about my difficult upbringing and my meeting and marrying Alicia and the notion that I'd been saved, but all anyone wanted to talk about was the drugs.

"You haven't been saved," she said. She looked bitterly at Alicia. "And if you're living like this, then *neither* of you are truly saved."

I have to admit to a little anger when these kinds of things happened. It was in that anger that people like this would always manage to confuse me—to make me believe that my relationship with Jesus wasn't what I believed it to be. The frustration I knew was substantial, but they were really getting to Alicia. At first, she suggested that we stop going, but I could see the true problem, so I told her that she should attend the meetings without me. Whenever I was feeling left behind, I would call my brother and he would remind that that, even though I was still messing up with the drugs, I was still saved.

"But they're telling Alicia that the only way she can accept Jesus is if she divorces me," I said on one such occasion.

"You've got to be kidding me," my brother said.

"I'm not kidding. It's only been three months we've been together, and they want her to end it."

"She's not seriously considering it, is she?"

I didn't really know how to answer the question. I wanted to believe that she wasn't, but there was that darker part of me that believed it was possible. And who could've blamed her? I had told her countless times that I would clean up my act, and here I was still using.

"You need to get out of that place," my brother suggested.

So that's what we did. We left all the negativity behind and decided to worship on our own for a while. This way, we could be free of outside opinions as we tried to reassemble our confidence in our marriage and in our faith.

We decided that part of the process should be to spend more time with Alicia's friends, but I never really fit in with them. I guess it was the opposing influences that I always seemed to bring to the table. There I was, this scruffy, not-exactly-recovering cokehead with a hoodlum past on the one hand, and a guy who wouldn't stop talking about his faith on the other. I think my steadfast refusal to speak about anything except through the lens of my religion was a bit of overcompensation for the sins I knew I was still committing. I guess I figured that the louder and harder I spoke about Jesus, the more it would overshadow the evil I still carried.

Even if I did think myself a true believer at the time, no one seemed to buy it. That just made me dig in further.

One night, we had a few couples over for dinner, and somehow the topic of abortion came up. I was passionate in my stance against it, so I took a knife and brought it into the dining room.

"What if you were pregnant and I stabbed you?" I asked of one of my wife's oldest friends in the world.

As the revulsion crossed every face in the room, I couldn't help but note how similar this moment felt to one from my past. I could still see my mother there with that knife, could still picture my brother wrestling it away. In the faces of the people who would never understand me, I found understanding about my own history. I was doing what I could to escape, but there was still a monster inside me.

Clearly the dinner was a disaster, but that was just the first of many. One after another, Alicia's friends started disappearing from her life, and it was all because I was so dogmatic. I was an angry born-again, and on top of that, someone who was still disappearing to do cocaine.

So there I was trying to figure out how to be a better and less aggressive Christian while my wife was just trying to hold our social life together. I still don't understand how she ever had the kind of patience it must have taken to stay with me. It's not like I was contributing much to the relationship other than my overwhelming charm, either. I was working an entry-level position, making a mere $15,000 a year, while Alicia was selling copiers for Pitney Bowes to the tune of $50,000 a year. It might have bothered me that she made more than three times my salary if I hadn't buried myself so deeply in what I thought was righteous indignation.

For some reason, my career started to take off, even if I wasn't paying full attention to the ride. At a company called CRT, word got around that I had a healthy relationship with numbers. I've always been gifted with math, but in a financial setting, my ability to quickly calculate numbers in my head made me uncommonly valuable. I guess that's why people started recommending me as a candidate to interview for the position at CRT. Of course I was excited about the opportunity to interview, but deep down, I was nervous because I knew it would lead to people asking about my résumé and education—or lack thereof, as it were.

Imagine my surprise when my interview landed me the opportunity to fly to Chicago for a follow-up meeting with the higher-ups in the company. I hadn't flown many times before, so on the plane, I was nervous to begin with. It didn't help that I spent the whole flight thinking about how there was no way on God's earth I would ever manage to weasel my way into this job. I knew I'd have the charm and the presentation to make a good impression, but one look at my record and it would be all over. If they asked for a high school diploma or college transcript, for instance, I'd have had nothing to give them. Forget about my criminal record if my true-fake name ever came to light.

The plane touched down at O'Hare and I hopped a train into midtown Chicago, where that fair city keeps the center of its trading activity. My employer's hub was located in a glimmering skyscraper among a sea of stone and glass. Inside, everything was marble and wood and everyone alarmingly chipper. It didn't take me long to realize that the good cheer probably came from how rich everyone had made themselves.

I felt like an imposter as I told the pretty lobby receptionist why I had come. She beamed and explained how I could make my way up to the top floor to find the interview room. As she punched in the number to announce my arrival, I felt a rush of adrenaline that both invigorated and calmed me. I had spent the whole trip thinking about what this job would do for my life and Alicia's, but now I remembered that this was merely one opportunity in what I was somehow sure would be a lifetime of them. Looking back, I think it was one of those rare moments where you feel God's hand on your shoulder, guiding you. Whatever the case, I felt all kinds of all right as the pretty secretary motioned me toward the elevators.

In the interview room, there were five serious men in suits. Behind them was a panorama of floor-to-ceiling windows and a stunning view of Lake Michigan beyond. It might have been an intimidating sight if I hadn't been feeling so completely reassured. The men let me know that they would be interviewing me one at a time. It seemed to me that most of them felt like they had more important places to be. I guess they were busy people about to go trade, so they preferred to keep the matter brief.

The first four interviewers treated me like a new acquaintance. They made small talk designed to get to know me, then basically just wished me luck with the rest of the interviews. I guess the effort was just to make sure I wasn't a complete knucklehead. With every passing interview, I became more confident that this meeting was just a formality. Everyone seemed like they were just welcoming me into the fold. And no one had even sniffed at my education.

Then came the last interview. Unlike the first four, this interviewer wasn't a trader. He was a spindly little oddball from human resources. I use the term *oddball* in the most endearing sense here, as well. He wore a cardigan sweater under his suit jacket, and glasses so round and large they obscured half his face. The weight of them kept causing them to fall down the bridge of his nose, so every few seconds or so, he would have to shove them back into place. I found myself wondering what sort of need or sense of fashion would compel a man to wear glasses so unnecessarily gigantic.

"So," he said, sounding strangely aloof, "you're Joseph Adevai."

With the way he accentuated the confirmation of my name, I knew a brief moment of panic. Had this man somehow discovered that I had another alias? Would all my hopes come crashing down on the back of one Joseph Carlucci?

"That's right," I said, arching a brow.

The HR man shuffled through some papers, then leaned back and crossed an ankle over his knee. He took a long, slow breath through his nose before tenting his fingers in front of his lips. He suddenly looked like a psychiatrist, and he sounded like one too. "Tell me, Joseph," he said breathily, "what *motivates* you?"

"What motivates me?" I repeated.

He nodded.

I'm not sure how I answered, but it must have satisfied him because he moved on to his next existential question.

"Where do you see yourself in five years?"

These are the kinds of questions for which most interviewees spend time beforehand preparing answers, but as wildly unfocused as I remained in those days, such big ideas hadn't ever occurred to me. I don't know how I answered that one, either, but I'm sure it sounded trite.

My interviewer didn't even bat an eye as he violently shifted gears. "Let's say you were on the trading floor," he said. "Can you picture that for me?"

"Sure," I said with a nod.

"Let's say you were on the trading floor and you saw someone making a trade that wasn't legal." He slid his glasses back on his nose and sniffled. "What would you do?"

"What would I do?"

He just stared at me as if willing me to answer. When I didn't at first, he added, "I'm just trying to see if we can figure out what guides your moral compass."

I can't remember ever being more uncomfortable in a professional setting. I was so confused by the mention of my moral compass, but at the same time, I knew the answer completely. The trouble was that I didn't know if the answer would endear me or ostracize me in this man's eyes. "I get it from Jesus Christ," I wanted to say, but I didn't know whether it would be acceptable to say it.

It's a weird, harrowing thing, loving God and your savior and feeling like you have to keep that love secret. I wrestled with that crisis long enough for my interviewer to take on one of those faces that says he suspects you're about to hand him a platter of platitudes. But then, just as he drew a breath to encourage an answer, I gave him the only one that made sense to me.

"This is an important interview for me," I said. "So more than anything, I just want to be open and honest."

"I think that would be for the best," my interviewer said, sounding genuinely pleased and surprised.

I shifted forward in my chair. "Well, I recently put my faith in Jesus Christ, so I guess you could say I get my moral compass from God."

The expression I saw from the HR man was unlike any I'd ever seen in another person. It was a combination of shock, and either delight or revulsion. It's difficult to explain how both delight and revulsion can seem to reside on the same face at the same time, but there it was. I don't know; maybe it was the enormous glasses that made it possible. Or maybe my interviewer had never heard a more honest answer. No matter what caused the look, the only interpretation I could manage caused my fear to return. Clearly this guy thought I was a Jesus freak who would try to evangelize him.

"Okay," he said simply. "That's all I need to know."

And then the interview abruptly ended.

As I exited the room and made my way, alone, out of the building, I wallowed in self-pity. I just couldn't believe I had mentioned my faith in an interview setting. As far as I was concerned, in this den of finance located in the glimmering heart of a great American city, there was no way a man who loved Jesus was getting a job.

I had reminded myself throughout the interview process that this was just an opportunity, and that many more would come along if this one didn't work out, but now that I could see that opportunity slipping away, I felt the weight of failure slowly stepping on me. I didn't want to think about what I would tell Alicia.

At the same time, I was also certain that I had done the right thing in God's eyes. I knew that there was no sense in compromising who I was just because I wanted a better job. God would provide, as far as I was concerned.

Then it hit me. Up to that point, many people had tried to tell me that I wasn't really born again because of the way I continued to behave. But back in that interview room, I had openly and willingly professed my faith in God. Even though I knew it stood a good chance of costing me a high-paying job, I wore my love of Jesus like a badge of honor. If that wasn't born again, I didn't know what was.

It's a strange feeling to walk out of a place with a gloomy sense that you've failed, but also that you're full of this light, fluttering sense of triumph. I had lost and won at the same time. I might not get the job and all the perks that came with it, but I had still taken a giant step forward in my life.

Back home, I tried to let the air out of Alicia's hope balloon slowly. When I returned to work, I didn't bother asking anyone for any updates from the home office. I just waited to see whether anyone would bother letting me know I'd been passed over.

Then one day, a guy named Richie Law strode in with a big grin on his face. "Well, Joe," he said, "When do you want to start?"

By then, I'd worked myself into so much doubt about the job interview that it took me a moment to piece together what he was talking about. "Start what?" I said.

Law gave me a confused look. "You do remember flying to Chicago for a job interview, right?"

I chuckled. "Of course."

"So I'm saying you got the job, and I'm asking you when you want to start."

My eyes went wide. My heart soared. My hands felt numb. My mind reeled in thanks to God. "I'll start now!" I heard myself saying.

"Well congratulations," Law said, making to leave my cubicle.

"Hey, Richie?" I called after him.

He stopped and turned back.

"How'd I get this job?" I asked. "I mean . . ."

"The Jesus thing?" Law finished for me.

"Yeah, I mean, everyone in Chicago was really nice, but I never thought they'd be able to look past my being born again."

Law shrugged. "Are you kidding? All those guys in Chicago are born again. Something like seventy percent of the company is born again."

My mouth must have been hanging open, because Law laughed. "I know, right? Looking at our office here in New York wouldn't give you that impression."

He was right. Most of the people in the New York office didn't like each other. Everyone seemed to be out for themselves, just trying to make a buck, no matter the expense on their relationships, godly or otherwise.

"Yeah, we might not be so spiritual out here," Law continued, "but the company was founded by four guys in Chicago who were Christians. They pretty much surrounded themselves with like minds."

"But how many Christians are there in the New York office?"

Law made a face and raised his index finger as if to start a list. "Well, there's you . . ." And then he stopped and smiled.

So that's how my love of God landed me a new job, a hefty raise, and an opportunity for bonuses that had the chance to double my salary. The company offered me an opportunity to join a mock trading class, as well, which allowed me a chance to see what it was like to trade in the pit. At the time, I was still a clerk sending signals from the floor to the pit while millions of dollars changed hands every minute. I wasn't in the game yet, but I felt like I had what it took to play. So I joined one of the classes.

The first session, I just watched as everyone screamed and

barked over their trades. I didn't want to scream and bark anything stupid, so I just observed. Every now and then, one of the experienced traders would pipe in and mix it up, I guess just to see if anyone had any idea how to think on their feet. Through it all, I kept my eyes open and my mouth shut.

By the second class, it was clear that most of the people who had been doing all the yelling hadn't learned much of anything because they were too busy wearing out their voices. But with all the watching I'd been doing, I felt like I was starting to understand what was going on. The yellers were making plenty of noise, but almost no money.

"You're all a bunch of knuckleheads," the traders would say after we had presented our numbers at the end of each class. They said many other less savory things in their efforts to coax some real production out of our class, but I won't list any of them here.

It was during the third class that I started to see the pattern. I spent much of that class watching the teachers. When one of them would say to buy something, everyone would try and buy it like a herd. This was the same kind of behavior I had observed in the pits during my time as a clerk. My classmates didn't seem to have a clue. They would just holler about buying whenever someone else told them to buy.

So I let them follow their herd. While they were buying stuff in one corner, I walked over to the other corner, where another trader was quietly offering other stuff. Little by little, I would buy from the teacher who was least active in the trading at the moment. Then, when the order came in to buy the less popular stuff, I had huge holdings in the asset and made millions.

In this way, I moved to the head of the class.

It only took a few more sessions before even the top traders in the company started to take notice. Then word came down that I was ready for the trading floor. They gave me a badge and turned me loose on the board of the New York Mercantile Exchange. These were twelve men serving as the ruling body of trading in the city, and slowly I pieced together that they needed to vote me into the community before I could ever make a real trade.

I felt every bit as nervous going into this meeting as I had going into my interview in Chicago—particularly since I figured my religious conviction would be of no consequence here. Standing before the twelve members of the board felt a little like standing in front of a jury at trial, as well. Unfamiliar with the process, I had no idea what was going on. What I did notice was that all twelve of them had a copy of the same thick folder. As they reviewed my record, they each went through it page by page and looked up at me like, "You've got to be kidding me with this guy."

"There are pages and pages of moving violations in here," one of them sniped.

Before I could explain myself, another one chimed in, "You worked at a pizzeria? Who *are* you?"

One after another, they tore me down, destroying my character and all hope I had for ever gaining legitimacy in this business. I was crushed to the point where I could hardly speak my replies to their questions. It seemed to me that I had a couple of supporters on the board, but they were far outweighed by the conviction of the few who didn't like what they saw.

"Mr. Adevai," one of them said, removing his glasses in a condescending way, "as long as I'm a member of this board, you'll never be a member of the New York Mercantile Exchange."

The meeting left me more depressed than I had been since the debacle with Alan. The thing about being addicted to a drug is that the way you get there and the impediment to your getting out come from the same place: doubt. That old crippling doubt returned to me after my interview. I had spent so much time trying to pull myself out of the gutter. I'd married the right woman, gotten a decent job that offered me chances to advance, started going to church, and had been born again. Even despite all that, I suddenly felt like that kid carting pizzas and snorting lines. I thought I would never break through that wall—that I would never amount to anything more than a clerk scraping together just enough to get by. I'd never be able to afford to help Alicia start the family she wanted.

As always, it was Alicia who provided me perspective. "So the only thing standing in your way is your moving violations?" she asked.

I put my head in my hands and my elbows on the kitchen table. She set her hand on my back and gave it a gentle pat.

"Only the moving violations," I said with an air of sarcasm. It seemed to me that Alicia had no idea how big the problem was.

She shrugged. "Well then, just go get them cleaned up."

The laugh that came to me was born just as much of derision as it was of relief. On the one hand, it was funny to me that Alicia thought it was such an easy fix. On the other hand, I could see that she was right: It was the only fix available to me. Regardless, the laugh was cathartic, and it at least cleared my mind enough to see how lucky I was to have someone so supportive and insightful in my life.

In January of 1988, I trudged into the Department of Motor Vehicles in Staten Island with a mind to clean up my history and open the door to my future. By now, the digging from the New York Mercantile Exchange board had unearthed the connection between Joseph Adevai and Joseph Carlucci. I had thought about trying to fight the notion that I was the latter, but both men had the same Social Security number, so I knew it would be no use. I'd made my bed. Now it was time to lie in it.

"So you're here to do what now?" the clerk asked me incredulously. I got the sense that she didn't get many requests like mine in any given day.

"I'm here to cover all my outstanding tickets," I said. "But to do that, I'm going to need a list of my violations."

She chuckled. "You get a lot of tickets?"

"You have no idea," I said with a smile.

For some reason, that seemed to take the humor out of her. She glared at me like I'd just insulted the picture of her kids she kept tacked to the corkboard on the wall of her cubicle.

"Would it be possible for you to print out a list of my violations?" I asked her gently.

With a sigh, she punched in a few commands and the printer started roaring. Back then, the DMV still used those printers that spit out their documents on those rolls of paper with the perforated edges. I stood there at the head of the cagey line, just listening as the printer kept humming and humming. With every passing minute and every piling roll of paper, I felt like I was getting buried deeper into my past. The violations just kept coming. It took over an hour for the printer to finally finish the job. By the time it was over, it was clear to everyone in the room that they were graced by the presence of one of the true champion scofflaws of both New York City and state.

My hands were quivering as I took my bulky stack of broken laws over to a chair in the corner of the depressing room and started adding up the numbers in my head. I'd never had a gift for obeying the law in my youth, but I'd always had a gift for numbers, so it didn't take me long to settle on a total. It all added up to just south of $75,000.

When I brought the figure home to Alicia, I expected her to have a heart attack, but her true reaction was even more surprising. I was amazed by how calm she was. It made me see how completely her faith in God had changed her.

She told me that she trusted God to provide a solution for us. "And besides," she said, "I believe in you."

That floored me. It was the first moment in my life when I saw someone truly believing in me. Sure, Alicia had taken a risk by marrying me in the first place, but here she was putting faith in me to do the right thing and to find a solution. No one but my wife had ever been willing to do that before. There is no way to describe how uplifting that moment was for me. It filled me with determination to come through for my family.

The problem was that, from a financial perspective, I had few options. Eventually I found an elderly lawyer who agreed to help me for a mere $300—probably because he was past retirement age and was really just taking on work like this to kill time. We went before a judge, where my attorney managed to work out a deal in a few quick conversations I couldn't quite hear from my position at the defendant's table.

It seemed like a long while that they were in conversation. My nerves were shot as the old man shuffled back to me. I tried to read something of the outcome in his expression, but he kept a blank face.

"Well, I think we're going to be all right," he said softly as he took his place beside me.

"You think?" I said.

He gave a slow nod, then motioned for me to pay attention to the judge.

"Mr. Adevai," the judge said, pausing as if trying to come up with words adequate to describe my mile-long record. He was a stern man with heavy eyebrows and a jowly chin. "I have to tell you that in the fifteen years I've been sitting this bench, I've never seen another offender with a record even close to this extensive."

"Thank you, Your Honor," I said stupidly.

"That wasn't a compliment." He shook his head, and I thought I heard him chuckle. "It's my understanding that you have taken steps recently to turn your life around. Is that so?"

"Yes, sir," I said. "I've gotten married. I have a steady job. And I'm Christian now, so—"

"That's all good and well," he interrupted, "but I need some assurance that you're putting these vehicular problems of yours behind you."

I nodded, my mind suddenly going blank. It wasn't until I felt the nudge from my lawyer that I finally managed to speak up. "Oh, yes, Your Honor," I stammered. "I'm on the straight and narrow now."

It was a funny thing to hear myself say that out loud. There was a time when I would have laughed at the notion, but now it was funny only because it was true. I had every intention of living a clean life from that point forward. The intention was so sudden and so genuine that it surprised even me.

The judge must have interpreted something of a heartfelt truth in the words, because he begrudgingly agreed to drop my fines from $75,000 to $14,000. At the time, that was still an astronomical sum for me to have to try and come up with, but I was in any case grateful to have been spared the fortune that was the remaining $61,000.

"Thank you, Your Honor," I said as my eyes welled up with tears. "I can't tell you what a relief it will be to put my past behind me."

"See that you do," he said, banging the gavel and sending me and my old lawyer on our way.

I was so overwhelmed with gratitude about the ruling that it wasn't until I got outside the courthouse that it occurred to me that I still had to come up with $14,000 I didn't have. This meant I would have to go to Alicia with a good news/bad news scenario, and given that our last conversation had ended with me as the villain, I wasn't all that excited at the prospect of hitting her with that gigantic number.

She went white as a sheet when I told her how much money I owed. Such was her shock that she actually sat down as if suddenly too weak to stand.

"But this is good news, honey," I said. "Fourteen thousand is a whole lot better than seventy."

It took her a while to answer, because she was quivering so

hard. She had her hands folded demurely in her lap. When I set my hand on them, they felt cold.

"It's not that," she said finally. "It's just the number fourteen thousand." She trailed off, unable to finish the thought.

"It's still a lot of money, I know, but we can—"

"I got my bonus today," she interrupted.

My heart skipped. "Yeah? And?"

She looked rather nauseated as she drew a breath to reply. "The check was for fourteen thousand, five hundred dollars."

My eyes went wide. The first thought that came to me was that God provides. There was no other way to explain how the sums had been so perfectly aligned. This bonus would cover my tickets while still leaving Alicia a few hundred dollars to spend on herself. My second thought was that I was the luckiest man alive.

"Wow," I said, trying to be coy. "That's a lot of copiers you sold."

"I had a good fourth quarter," she said dismissively.

We stared at each other for a long while then, each of us measuring up who would be the first to voice the obvious connection. There was no denying the convenience in the numbers, but there was also no denying that, if I asked her for this money, I would be taking an entire year's worth of work from her—and as a proud career woman, I knew that would cut her deep. For as long as I had known her, she had thought of her job and her skill at that job as a major part of her identity. Here I was staring her in the face, about to ask if I could please have all the rewards for the hard work she had committed all year long.

I felt wretched about it, but after all, fortune favors the bold. "I don't want to ask you for that money," I said. "And I'm sure you don't want to give it. But the only way I'm going to get past my history—and the only way I'm ever going to advance at work—is with that money."

She shuddered through a sigh.

"Besides," I said, trailing off because I really hated myself for where I was going with this, "we're married now. So whatever is mine is yours, and whatever is yours is mine."

When she heard that, Alicia set the new world record for batting her eyes. I could see that I had upset her, but at the same time, I could see that she agreed with me. We had committed to each other through thick and thin. This just happened to be one of the thin periods, and I happened to be the guy bringing it about. If our roles had been reversed, I wouldn't have hesitated to give her the money. And in the end, she didn't hesitate either.

After she took a couple hundred dollars to splurge on a few things for herself, she gave me the rest. I could see her reluctance—and how could I blame her? It wasn't that long ago that I had been a drug-abusing multiple felon, and I was still occasionally sniffing around the fringes of drug abuse. But ultimately, we both knew that what we were buying wasn't a cleaner past for me; we were buying a better future.

I had never been more excited than I was when I paid off that debt. It didn't just feel like a weight had lifted from my shoulders, but rather, that a dark film had peeled back from my vision. Everything looked brighter. Everything made me happier. My world had become a better place.

Under that new, brighter outlook, I went to my boss—the one

who had been such a rain cloud over my chances of advancing—and showed him my expunged record. "Can you get me into the meeting now?" I asked.

He hemmed and hawed. "I'll have to look into it," was the prevailing sentiment.

The committee only met monthly, so every time my boss missed the window, I would go back to him and ask again. Month in and month out, he had a new reason he couldn't get me in. Eventually it became apparent that he wasn't really trying to help me in the matter.

Fortunately, around this time, I had also learned about fasting—I write "fortunately" because, with the way I was feeling about my boss at the time, I was either going to beat him up and get thrown in jail or focus all my frustration on praying and fasting. For three days, I fasted while working on the trading floor, and on the third day of the fast, I felt the Holy Spirit come over me. I found peace that everything with work was going to be okay. I was no longer frustrated about paying off the tickets with nothing to show for it. I started seeing things with God's eyes.

The next time I saw my boss, I was much more casual about the matter. "Is there anything going on with the board?" I asked.

"As a matter of fact, yes," he said. "You're going before the board at the next meeting."

The next time I stood before the NYMEX committee, the chairman who had given the vow that I would never be a member of the exchange had moved on to another board. That fact, combined with the knowing looks or winks I was receiving from a few of the other members of the board, gave me a sense that everything would be fine. Laughably bad driving record or no, I had developed my share of friendships in the industry, and people knew my character. I didn't curse or try to rob people or look for angles and ethical gray areas. I was a straight shooter and a hard worker, and on the trading floor, those are two qualities plated in gold.

Sure enough, I passed and received my trading badge. I felt as if my debts to the state and to my wife had been paid, at least figuratively. Soon I would earn enough money to return Alicia's bonus to her. In the meantime, now we had a future—and in that future, we saw a family.

CHAPTER SEVEN

The Midst of Trial

IN APRIL OF 1988, Alicia delivered the greatest news I had ever received. She was pregnant. This news could not have left me feeling more joyful or more terrified. I had never experienced those two emotions side by side before, so it was a new kind of sensation for me. On the one hand, I couldn't wait to be a father. That thought alone made me feel like maybe I had finally turned that corner as a human being. I was more confident in my faith, and I felt good about work. The terror came from the notion that Alicia's pregnancy started the clock ticking on the deadline for when we would need to be able to get by on just one salary. I was making good money at the time, but not nearly enough to completely replace Alicia's healthy paychecks.

This new sense of urgency caused me to put the pedal down on the trading floor. My company had started me out in a pit of traders working in heating oil and gasoline. In the main pit, hundreds of thousands of crude oil contracts traded hands every day, but the pit where they had placed me encountered no more than a couple hundred trades. This was fine, but if I was going to make enough money to allow Alicia to stay home with our firstborn, I would need to get aggressive.

I started off by doing the same trade every day with this one customer who was trying to bury me. He sold me options, but I wouldn't take too much at first. I made some calls to people upstairs, and we kept buying because this one seller was selling cheap. It was like someone selling milk for a dollar when it was in the grocery store for three. The customer was trying to run me over and then buy it back from me when I got scared. This tactic might have intimidated most rookies, but I was confident.

As it stood, the options I purchased set my company back $500,000, but I was able to trade around it with other customers, so it didn't look like there was such a huge deficit. Then one day, the price came down again, so I went to my supervisor and told him we should buy even more.

"Fine," he said, "but if it comes back to bite us, you're the one taking the heat."

The months dragged by after that, but still I kept making that same trade. I knew that if the price of gas and oil went up, my company would make a mint, and it would open up the opportunity for Alicia to stay home with our child. There was of course a flip side to the strategy, and that flip side would have ruined us, but I felt confident that I was doing what was right and that God was on my side.

That next year, Super Bowl Sunday came on January 22, 1989. I remember the date—and just about every detail from that day—for a few key reasons, and they had nothing to do with the game. I was at a friend's house in Union, New Jersey. The game featured the Cincinnati Bengals and the San Francisco

49ers, which meant I didn't have more than a passing interest because I've always been a huge Giants fan. The game was not without its intrigue, though, because it all came down to the last drive. It was 16-13 Bengals, with two minutes left, but the 49ers had the ball at the twenty-yard line and Joe Montana—one of the greatest comeback specialists of all time—at quarterback. My friends and I could sense a classic finish brewing.

That's when I got the call from Alicia.

"Hey, honey," I said. "The game's winding down. I should be home soon, and—"

"I think it's now," she cut in.

My heart started to race. "You think what's now?"

I could hear that she was breathing heavily. "The baby's coming."

It's difficult to explain what happens to a man's mind when he hears his firstborn child is on its way. He becomes laser focused and clearheaded, but at the same time, a numb kind of fear grips him. It's a strange sensation. I could hardly feel my fingers as I held on to the phone, but at the same time, my mind was working quicker and clearer than it had in years. I quickly calculated that I would have plenty of time to get to her mother's house in Montclair so I could drive her to the hospital.

"Okay," I said. "I'll come get you."

At the same time, I wasn't yet a father, so I hadn't yet experienced what it means to be truly responsible. In many ways, a man doesn't become a man until he holds his child in his hands for the first time. I'm embarrassed to write this, but I didn't leave the party right away. I figured I had plenty of time to get to Montclair. I had always heard that births could take twenty-four hours or more. Besides, we had already had a couple of false alarms to that point. So it didn't seem right to turn my back on a game that was sure to have a memorable finish.

I stayed and watched to the end. Sure enough, Montana came through. I was so enthralled by the heroics of it all that I told myself that if Alicia had a boy, we would name him Joe Montana Adevai.

When it was over, I hopped into my car and squealed toward Montclair.

"This is real," I said when I saw Alicia. She looked pale and nervous, and she was breathing with purpose. "This isn't another false alarm."

"No, this is not a drill," she said adamantly.

It was at that moment that I finally started feeling appropriately terrible about staying to watch the end of a football game while my wife was in labor. I took out my frustration on the highway. Once we had Alicia belted in, I absolutely flew down the turnpike.

The hospital was in Perth Amboy, which wasn't exactly the closest to our location. Since we were alone in the car, I kept an eye on the digital clock on my dashboard to time her contractions. They were already only five minutes apart. Between glances at the clock, I was trying to focus on the road, but the next thing I knew, she was taking off her seat belt and turning around in the front seat.

"What are you doing?" I hollered.

She was in too much pain to answer. Instead, she doubled over into a kneeling position and leaned into the back seat. Her next contraction came only three minutes later.

We approached a tollbooth, and despite my newly cleared driving record, I blew right through. "My wife's pregnant!" I yelled back from my open window. I did this at every other tollbooth after, and we never picked up a police escort.

Forty minutes later, we had made it to the hospital. At first, the nurses shuffled us into the delivery room and left us alone. But in a matter of minutes, Alicia had a massive contraction, and when I looked over, I saw the baby's head.

"Help!" I called as I ran into the hallway. "Somebody! The head is coming out!"

I stood there, looking wildly from side to side for some sign of someone who might help us. There was no way I was going back in there alone because I'd just seen more than I could handle already.

After a team of doctors rushed in, it was a matter of only fifteen minutes before Alicia had given birth to our first child, a girl we named Alexandra. With her full head of hair, her perfect nose, and her big eyes, she was the most adorable baby I had ever seen. I could hardly believe I had a baby girl. I was so overcome with emotion and exhaustion that the nurses set me up on a stretcher and asked if I needed an IV. I passed on the fluids and just rested for a while, wallowing in bliss.

My mother was not among the procession of family members that came to visit the baby after we returned home, but that was the least of my concerns. Chief on my mind was the notion that I still wasn't making enough money for Alicia to leave her job permanently. Those risky deals I was doing at work suddenly loomed larger. What if oil prices plummeted?

I'd have cost my company hundreds of thousands of dollars and myself a job at a time when we could least afford it.

Fortunately, we caught a break—although I use the word *fortunately* lightly here because there is no way to put an entirely positive spin on the disaster that precipitated the break. It was March 24, 1989, when the Exxon Valdez oil spill changed my life. The commodity options I had been buying on the cheap wound up netting my company $7 million. The bonus I received from those trades came to just under $30,000, and it came just over two months after the birth of my daughter and a year after Alicia had given me her bonus check to pay off my moving violations. My bonus was the first significant amount of money I ever earned outside of selling cocaine. And unlike a single dime I had made before it, that bonus made me feel right inside and with the world.

When it came to the baby, Alicia did the bulk of the work. Occasionally I would change a diaper, but there was no comparison to how amazing Alicia was. She was stronger and more capable than I ever could have imagined a woman being.

Not long after, I used one of my bonuses for the down payment on a house on Myrtle Street in Edison. The house was tiny, with a first floor featuring nothing more than a kitchen and living room, and up the little staircase, there were just two bedrooms in a loft area with slanted ceilings. Many nights, I would wake up and bump my head. The next room was plenty large for Alex's crib, but she was the only one of us with enough room. Since there were no closets, Alicia bought herself a dresser and armoire for her clothes. My clothes I just kind of flung wherever it made sense to fling them.

After we settled in, Alicia's aunt told us about this start-up church in Edison called the Christ Community Church. The place met in the living room of the pastor's house. There were only five people there when we first showed up with baby Alex. Pastor Dennis Cahill greeted us, then introduced us to a bunch of delightfully laid-back people. It was exactly what I expected of a church that met inside a house. When I heard the tinkling of a piano, I peeked into the dining room to find a man pounding the keys of a baby grand.

"That's John Bevilacqua," the pastor told me.

I laughed under my breath because the way John played reminded me of Lurch from *The Addam's Family*. Later, when I met John, I found we had a quick rapport. He had a daughter a little older than Alex, so we had plenty in common.

After only a few visits, I had already established myself as the conspicuously loud one among the group. This was the first time I'd ever been so open about my praising. I would like to say that my volume was owed to how good I felt about myself and the life Alicia and I had made together, but the truth was that I owed my vigor to the notion that I felt like if I could party hard at the night club, then I should party harder in church. Plus, I guess I figured the harder I worshiped, the less likely it was for anyone else to find out I was a former drug dealer and burglar. I didn't want to open up about the life I'd led.

After attending the church for a while, the pastor suggested that we start holding our services at a local school. We needed to fill more seats if we were going to make that happen, so we all agreed to contribute to a phone campaign. We made close to ten thousand phone calls, and I made at least three thousand of them. I was always trying to go the extra mile at that church, a factor also derived from my party hard/worship harder mindset. Besides, the more calls I was making, the less opportunity I had to do something or meet with someone that would cause a relapse.

As a result of the campaign, 180 people showed up to the first service at Washington Elementary School. I was so excited about the turnout that I helped set up and clean up with a smile on my face. I was all in. Unfortunately, not everyone else in that first crowd felt the same way. After a few weeks, the numbers had dwindled to forty.

Eventually, Alicia and I decided that it was time to get even more involved, so we volunteered to host a group in our home. The twelve people assigned to join us took up our whole living room and dining room. This was our first opportunity to lead a session of spiritual exploration, and I have to admit that I had caught the bug from the moment it started. I was so enamored with leading others in scripture that I knew I had to volunteer in that capacity however I could. So Alicia got involved in the women's ministry, and when the church started talking about starting a youth group, I quickly threw my name into the ring. Anything Pastor Cahill wanted, I did, and in the meantime, he encouraged me while I struggled with being a new Christian. He was an excellent pastor to have at that time in my life.

Nine months in, it was evident that the church needed help, especially in regard to worship music, so the church voted in an associate pastor named Rick Ravis. He did a great job leading worship, and we became fast friends. With all these new changes, the church decided to start an advisory board, and I was asked to be one of six members. We held meetings once a month, and as my first experience with church politics, I quickly realized that I didn't much care for them. While most people preferred to maintain the status quo, I always wanted to shake things up. This made for some heated discussions, and I couldn't ever quite get comfortable.

With the money I was making on the market, I started to realize that I had another avenue to contribute to the church. So I bought a sound system to aid our newly blossoming music segments. This turned out to be a nice blessing for the church, but another duty for me to attend to, as I was the only one who seemed to know how to set everything up. So for the next three years, it was my job to transport, set up, and take down the sound system every Sunday.

And through all this, I was still occasionally slipping into cocaine.

The guilt was overwhelming. Alicia never said a word to anyone. God bless her.

Then it happened one Thursday at an advisory board meeting. The conversation was completely banal; the other leaders were deciding whether we should get more toner or a copy machine, and it bothered me to be talking about something so trivial—or at least I thought that's what was bothering me.

In any case, I launched into a diatribe about how ludicrous it was to be talking about spending this kind of money on a copy machine when there was so much good work to be done in the world. I started to boil inside, but not for the reasons I thought I was boiling. "We're all a bunch of hypocrites," I heard myself saying. "Every Sunday, we talk about wanting to spread

the word, and here we are talking about how we can most effi-
ciently make copies of our flyers."

"What's your point, Joe?" someone said.

"My point is, would Jesus have used flyers?" By then, I could
feel how red my face had gone from the hollering. I could see
the wide eyes of all my colleagues. And it was like I was listening
to myself speak without having any real control over the words.
"See? Hypocrites." Then as I sat down and everyone mulled the
thought silently, it hit me. *You've got a lot of nerve calling them
hypocrites*, I thought. *You're snorting cocaine.*

It was then that I knew how everything I had been hiding
was about to be revealed. I had been living in the darkness long
enough. Now it was time to step into the light. I felt myself tear
up, and then the eyes started turning on me.

You shouldn't even be here, I thought. *You should go.* I actually
started to rise, but then another thought held me to my seat.
Unless you confess. A tear escaped over my cheek. *You have to
say it.*

Then the floodgates opened. I started to sob. I buried my
face in my hands and leaned forward. In time, I felt a comfort-
ing hand on my back. The room started spinning, and my heart
pounded as if it would leap from my chest. All at the same time,
I felt as if there was nothing I could do and that I knew there
was exactly one thing I could do. I had to unshackle myself
from the guilt. I had to be honest about my addiction publicly
for the first time.

"I'm doing cocaine," I said.

I don't know what kind of reaction I was expecting, but the
one I got was shock. I blew those poor people out of the water.

From the looks on a few of the faces, I could tell that some of these men wouldn't know what cocaine was if I'd smacked them in the face with a powdery brick of it. But it was the look on Pastor Cahill's face that made the crying return.

Apart from my sobbing, the room was silent.

I cried for what felt like an hour, but was in reality no more than a minute or two. It was the most painful, difficult admission I had ever made to anyone. I thought there would be no end to the agony. But then a strange thing happened. The silence started to feel less like judgment and more like a cleansing rain. I had shared my darkest secret with a room full of men I trusted, and I'm sure they were judging me, but that mattered less and less with each passing second. I had admitted my sin, and it felt as if the weight of the world had lifted from my shoulders.

It was Pastor Cahill who spoke first. "Okay," he said, sounding a little uncomfortable. "We've had a little bit of a turn in our meeting today. So let's do what we always do in times of trial. Let's pray."

I listened to my pastor lead them in prayer for my soul. They asked for my forgiveness and for guidance out of the dark. Through it all, I cried, but now my tears were not of pain, but rather, of hope.

When it was over, they told me that they respected me for being honest, but that they also couldn't allow me to continue on the advisory board. I understood the decision, and even agreed with it. My only fear was that I wouldn't be able to continue with this church. I had been helping out with the youth group, after all, and I would have to step down from that, too.

Eventually word would get out about why I was leaving all these leadership roles.

My guilt had gone, but now I knew shame. Guilt can make a man do terrible things, but when it comes to breaking him completely, there's nothing quite like shame. My breaking came in the familiar form of white powder, but also—of all things—in a game with the Staten Island Touch Tackle football league.

I'm not sure whether I didn't enjoy showing my face at church anymore, or if I really did care that much about the football league I would wind up playing with for twenty years, but after my admission to the advisory board, I started skipping out on church some Sundays so I could play football. My team was good—*championship* good—so I would occasionally use that as an excuse to leave church services early or even skip altogether. I went about my business in this way for over a month after that fateful day with the board. Then there came a week when my game was bumped to Monday night and I had no excuse to miss service.

That week, the sermon was about commitment—to God and to the church. For the first time since I'd turned my back on my faith, I could sense that God was speaking directly to me.

A few days later, I called my football coach and told him I couldn't play anymore. I caught some heat about that, and it was really difficult to quit in the end, given that it was such a deep connection with my old life. I had spent so many hours at summer practices, and so many years playing for a team that was high-profile enough to get my picture and a few write-ups of me in the paper. But ultimately I knew I had rid myself of as many of my distracting influences as I could. Unfortunately, I still had another fire that was much more threatening.

Despite my being a father and a supposed Christian now, I was still going out and partying from time to time. Usually, I would keep my benders to a single night, but one weekend shortly after I quit football, I went out on a Friday night and didn't come home until Sunday.

When I first showed my ragged face at the door that Sunday, Alicia wasted no time.

"I'm calling Pastor Cahill," she said.

Oh God, I thought through the hangover fog. *More guilt! Just what I need.*

The next thing I knew, I was in my basement next to my wife and sitting across from a pastor reading Psalm 51. Everyone was talking about cleansing me, and then suddenly I was having water dumped on my head.

"You are forgiven," Pastor Rick Davis said.

I started to try speaking through my tears. "But, Pastor, I—"

"God loves you," he interrupted. "God forgives you." He pointed at his Bible. "Look at David in this Psalm. He says, 'Wash me and I'll be clean.'"

It was then that I saw the meaning behind the ritual. It wasn't my stopping cocaine that would cleanse me; it was God who would cleanse me. The answer wasn't trying to force myself out of the gutter; the answer was to allow the Holy Spirit to lift me from the gutter. The difference might seem subtle at first, but to me, in that moment, it changed my life.

A few weeks later, I felt the urge to do coke as I was driving down Rockland Avenue on route to Staten Island. I knew this street as a place famous for having a house full of what most people thought was a "Jesus freak" cult. Meanwhile, just up the road there was a stretch of woods where people claimed devil worshippers would gather. So this was a very good-versus-evil kind of avenue. My heart reflected that same sort of turmoil. I wanted coke, and I knew that I was five minutes away from a place where I could get it. Before that cleansing in my basement, there would have been no question about the choice I would have made. I would have told myself that cocaine is fine for now as long as I promise to clean up my act after this one last time. But now I was filled with the Holy Spirit. Now I had the means to rise above it.

I pulled the car over, slapped my hands against the wheel a few times, and started giving myself a little pep talk. "You don't have to do this," I said, and that's the first time it ever occurred to me that it was true. It used to be that I told myself something like, "If you do this, you're going to pay for it later." That's a weak, ineffectual message compared to this one: "You don't have to do this, Joe," I said—and I was speaking the words, but it was almost like they were coming from outside of myself, as if they were coming from something much bigger than me. "You don't have to go. You can stop right now and turn around and wake up tomorrow and feel okay in your stomach and in your head and in your heart. You don't have to do this." And more importantly, it was as if God was telling me I didn't have to do this because He loved me.

That's all I heard, and it filled me with a rush I can't properly describe. With more confidence than I can ever remember feeling, I threw the car into drive, turned it around, and went home. I had never felt better, because for the first time since I could remember, I didn't feel like I had to do cocaine.

As I write this, I'm tearing up thinking about how I never did the drug again. That's miraculous in more ways than one—not the least of which being that most of the friends with whom I used to party either ended up in AA, NA, or dead, including two of my best friends, Richie and Biff, who died of AIDS they contracted from drug use. Some are still on coke to this day. Some still hang out at those same street corners, snorting cocaine at the age of fifty.

The next day, I went to church and praised like I had never praised before. It seemed to me that everyone present could sense the change I had just made in my life. And it wasn't long before they started to trust me again. They brought me back into leadership roles, and eventually I took over as the youth leader.

The role as youth leader was one of the most profound positions I have ever held, because many of the kids in that group were in the same kinds of messes I'd been struggling with my whole life. I taught them that they weren't alone in their struggle—that whenever they were feeling lost, God would guide them—and they taught me what it meant to minister—that whenever I was feeling lost, God would guide *me.*

When the church asked me to become an elder, I accepted the offer even though I dislike the word *elder.* I had dropped the cocaine and the guilt that came with it, but I still proved myself to be a pain at meetings. I refused to vote on things like toner and whether to get new chairs, and I found myself baffled every time the question came up about whether we should raise the pastor's annual salary by a measly 1 percent.

"I can't understand why anyone would want to be a pastor," I remember telling Alicia once. "They do so much work for so little in return. Their lives must be miserable."

"Oh, I know," Alicia said. "And I'd never want to be a pastor's wife, either. They always seem so subdued and depressed."

In that denomination, a pastor's wife didn't talk in front of a church, so we were left mostly to speculate about what she was going through and whether their family had enough to get by on the pastor's small budget.

After that conversation with Alicia, it became my goal to get the pastor the kind of raise that would allow him to live comfortably. I became something of a freelance financial liaison between the pastor and the congregation. I figured that if the people in my world were making so much money, it should be fine to give a spiritual leader $2,000 more a year. It all just seemed so ridiculous. Why vote to give that righteous family an extra thirty dollars per month when they were giving their lives to God? These were the kinds of people who would cleanse me in the basement during my time of darkness. How could we not reward that kind of commitment?

Around this same time, it was decided that the youth group should lead a church service. As the leader of the youth group, this meant that I would be given my first opportunity to preach. It's funny to look back on the way things developed for me in that church. Preaching had never really been a thought for me, but in many ways, the call to lead kind of fell in my lap. When they told me about the assignment, my first thought was, *There's no way that's going to work.* I had managed the announcements in front of the congregation a few times before, and every time, I was terrified—shaking like a dying leaf—and it was a proper disaster. I had no real desire to ever stand in front of a crowd again.

Pastor Rick didn't want to allow me out of it. He encouraged me to preach to the congregation. "Just pretend like you're talking to your youth group," he told me. "You don't ever have any trouble speaking to them, I hear."

He winked, for I think it had gotten to be a bit of a running line about what a windbag I could be with the kids.

So one Sunday, my breath short and my heart roaring, I stepped to the podium to lead a service. As a prop for my sermon, I wore my trading badge from the commodities pit. The badge bore the letters *JCL*, which as I explained, stood for "Jesus Christ is Lord." I could see that it surprised some of the people in the audience to hear that I rather literally wore my faith on my sleeve at work.

I based my sermon on 1 Corinthians 3, the passage about Paul planting seeds, Apollos watering those seeds, and God causing the growth. My interpretation was that this was God's way of telling us to be bold when representing Christ. I was indeed nervous throughout the talk, but after the service was over, I received nothing but positive feedback. And with that, I had caught the bug to preach.

In January of 1990, at the promise of almost four times my salary at the time, I made the leap with two other traders who started their own company called Saratoga Energy. The first eight months of work were good for the three of us, as I had made $1 million on a spectacularly good run of trades. Then Saddam Hussein decided to invade Kuwait, causing the price of oil to skyrocket and me to lose $250,000 in the blink of an eye. I was still up for the year, but I had never lost so much in a day, and in many ways, it soured me to the business.

And it would only get worse. For the next few months, whenever Saddam made a speech about blood in the streets, the price of oil would shoot up. Then later, he would say that he was hoping to make peace with the US, and the price would go down. He was bipolar—I was sure of it—and the markets reflected that same manic-depressive sensibility. Up to that point, I had always been a safe trader, but with that kind of volatility, safe traders don't make any money. So I decided to take a risk.

One day, I bought a hundred lots, which was equivalent to a hundred thousand barrels of oil. The moment I made the trade, I figured Saddam would say something stupid, and sure enough, fifteen minutes later, he made a speech that led to a $300,000 gain in one day. That was quite a high, but in reality, that last big gain was the beginning of the end for me as a trader. There's something strange that happens to a trader when he gets a taste of a big payoff. Any sensibility I used to have flew straight out the window. The rush I'd gotten from making a huge gain on a volatile market was the closest feeling to being high on drugs I had ever experienced. So I kept pushing the envelope. From late August of 1990 until October of that same year, my account gained another $3 million. During that time, I made $1.2 million in one day. The guys I was working with were so pleased that they didn't even know what to say to me.

Ah, but with the highest highs come the lowest lows. October was a rough month. By my birthday (October 31), my account had hemorrhaged its way down to negative $700,000 and I was walking around like the undead, I was so depressed. I could sense that I was about to get cut loose. After I begged for another chance, my employers switched me to a more liquid trading environment, which allowed me to get my account back up to a healthier number, but the chaos on the market that resulted from the Gulf War made it difficult to keep climbing for any extended period. I held on for almost exactly a year from that low point of my birthday, but in 1991, I lost my job. I was devastated. I went from golden boy to unemployed in just two short years.

By then, Alicia and I had had two more girls—Victoria and Jacqueline—so my on-again, off-again employment record that followed me around for the next couple of years was difficult for the family to bear. It got so bad that I eventually started working construction with some friends during the day and driving limos at night and on the weekends. After moving millions of dollars a day, it felt like a pretty giant step backward, but I did whatever I had to do because I had three kids and needed to keep money coming in.

Other opportunities to trade followed, but it was always the same story: I would start the year incredibly well, but then end it on a downslide and lose my job. It got to where I thought I was cursed. Looking back, I can see that it wasn't a curse at all: It was a blessing. It was God's way of telling me I was pursuing the wrong line of work. Some people might have gotten that message after just one disastrous year, but I guess I've always been hardheaded that way.

I guess Jesus got tired of waiting for me to come around, because I was on the trading floor one day when someone handed me a flyer advertising a weekly Bible study among some of the traders. I was excited about the prospect, so I met with Pastor Dan Stratton, the leader of the group. I found him in the crude oil pit, and he urged me to step in for a session.

"Wait," he said toward the end of the conversation. "You're a trader?"

I nodded, figuring that keeping the answer simple might be better than revealing what a hard-luck trader I had been of late.

He gave me an appraising look. "You know, I could use a good man like you. It's not often you find a trader who's also a Christian."

"Well, that's me through and through," I told him.

So that's how it came to be that Pastor Dan fronted me some money and I started trading again. Just like I always did, I made a couple hundred thousand dollars almost immediately, so my new backer was ecstatic.

It was 1993, and when October came around that year, I started to dread my usual turn of disaster, but that year, I would be blessed instead with the birth of my first son, Joey. When the doctors pulled Joey out and I saw that little stem, I screamed with joy. I love my three daughters dearly, but by then, I was ready for a boy.

Later, in the hallway, a couple of nurses stopped me and said, "Were you that guy screaming?"

I laughed as I explained myself. "I have three daughters already," I said. "The thought of another one was just too much to bear."

They chuckled and sent me on my way. I was still so excited that I ran from end to end of the hospital, just hollering about how I finally had a son.

As my family grew, I kept on with Pastor Dan. I was still up a couple hundred thousand by April of 1994, but I wasn't making much beyond that. Pastor Dan usually kept a wary eye on me, because by then I had told him about how volatile my career had been, but I guess by April he was feeling comfortable enough to let me do my thing because he took a ministry trip to Africa. While he was gone, OPEC made some decisions that dropped the price of oil from fourteen to thirteen dollars per barrel in a single day. I lost a ton with that decision, and then I compounded the issue by trying desperately to make it back. Long story short, I compounded my losses and wound up in the red by $70,000. Someone called Pastor Dan in Africa, and he told them to liquidate my position.

"That's not a great idea," I told the guy who delivered the news. "You'll more than double the losses if you drop me now."

"What can I do?" he said. "Dan was adamant."

"Can I get him on the line?"

The guy shrugged. "I'm sorry, Joe. You're out."

There are few times in my life where I would have rather been wrong, but that was one of them. By liquidating me then, Pastor Dan lost another $100,000. So I was on the hook to him for $170,000.

Pastor Dan could have done any number of things after a loss like that. I wasn't under contract, but he could have easily sued us or even come after our house. But I guess he understood where I was coming from.

"Look," I told him, "I messed up. But believe me when I tell you that I'll pay you back every penny."

I didn't have to pay him—I wasn't under any legal obligation to do so—but I knew it was the right thing to do. Alicia took it especially hard, given that we had a mortgage and four children to feed. It didn't help that several of the family and friends in our lives were telling her to divorce me after I lost all that money. These were the same people who had told her that she was making a mistake by marrying me in the first place. So now they had their righteous indignation to share. They would start sharing this opinion immediately after they learned I'd lost all that money, and they would continue sharing it for more than a year after that. For a while there, I couldn't help but kind of agree with their position. I hadn't done much more than fail in my career up to that point.

To Alicia's great credit, she listened to these people, and held her own concerns, but it was clear that she would never give in to the temptation to be rid of me. My wife could have divorced me and rid herself of the debt, but in the end, she never even considered it.

"Honey," I told her, "I know it's a hardship, but right now, I just feel like I have to do the right thing. I'm going to pay him back. Maybe it'll take me twenty years, but it's all I can do."

I don't know how she did it, but Alicia suffered through it all with me, and did it with a smile. She was always sweet but strong, always resolute in her support for me. First she had ushered me through my addiction to cocaine, then through my various crises of faith, and now through the highs and lows of being rich and poor again and again. I wish I had been able to endure this period of our lives with the same level head as my wife. But in truth, I yelled a lot and was wildly emotional. Before I fully accepted Christ as my calling, I carried around more insecurities than I can count.

In my view, what I needed was a new path. That path proved elusive at first, but eventually I figured out that, to move ahead, sometimes you have to change everything about what you're doing. I had a monstrous debt, and I knew that there was at least one way that I might be able to make fast money to pay it off, but something told me that my days of fast money on the trading floor were over.

It's not like I could have found a job on Wall Street at that point anyway. I had burned out my credit with just about everyone. So after my period of waffling and feeling sorry for myself finally ended, I took a job in John Bevilacqua's flooring business. I made a tenth of what I was making on the trading floor, and the work was hard, but at least it was honest work. To go from having my dream job as a trader to putting tile on the ground, sweeping up dust, and inhaling glue was a humbling experience. I felt like Joseph, who had his dreams, and then had his prison. It wasn't that John was putting me in prison—he was very generous with me—rather, the prison was in my mind. On nights and weekends, I drove a limo and hung out in airports, holding up signs for wealthy businesspeople coming and going. I thought about how foolish I would look if I ran into one of my friends from Wall Street. Every time I faced a doubt or insecurity like this, I thought about my wife and children, and that always gave me the strength to carry on. Between them and Jesus, I managed to keep scraping together paychecks without turning to drugs or otherwise straying from the path.

The jobs didn't pay much, but I would still send Pastor Dan one or two hundred dollars per month, just to let him know I was sincere about paying my debt. Meanwhile, I kept attending his Bible study and monthly revival meetings. I began to think that God allowed everything to happen because He wanted me to stick with Pastor Dan. It would have been the easiest thing in the world to avoid this man because I owed him money, but every time I saw him, rather than finding shame, I would feel invigorated by the challenge my debt to him represented. It was as if God was saying, "Whatever is the most difficult thing to do, that is what you must do."

For me, the most difficult thing I could imagine was scraping together a couple hundred bucks each month to give to a man whose Bible studies and revival meetings I was visiting weekly. It was especially tough whenever Pastor Dan would preach about how his biggest trial was losing all that money, but to his credit, he never pointed the finger at me for having been the guy who lost it.

Even though the sessions often made me feel terrible, I could sense that God wanted me there. Maybe it was because I needed that experience to learn more about humility, and also because it exposed me to a range of incredibly powerful speakers. Pastor Dan often invited in genuinely gifted guest speakers, and their words always inspired me to better myself as a man and as a preacher of the Word. Before those sessions, I used to think of God as constantly telling me to get my act together or He'd stomp me, but through those many talks, I came to understand that He loved me and wanted to bless me, if only I started doing the right things for myself and my family.

At the revivals, I encountered the Holy Spirit like never before. I saw people healed, and felt my heart lift to the heavens again and again. I brought many of my friends from Christ Community, even though they didn't necessarily share the same theology. I always marveled at how some of them were touched by God while others were freaked out by the spectacle of it all.

Around that same time, I decided that the only way I was going to get my family whole again was to find a job that paid me a higher salary. So I made a call to a Christian friend on Wall Street, told him I was broke, and asked him if there was anything he could do for me.

"Have you ever thought about becoming an OTC broker?" he asked me.

I hadn't. Really, as a trader, the thought had never occurred to me to work that side of the business, but it did seem like there was at least some opportunity to get ahead. I took a job with a $45,000 per year salary—which, coming from limo driving and flooring, felt like a fortune. On top of that, I would have the opportunity for bonuses.

The only trouble was that the company was new to the OTC brokerage industry, had an alcoholic for a CEO, and had no idea what they were doing. They kept giving me paychecks for getting my work done, but I could tell that there wasn't any money coming in. That's when I decided that enough was enough, and picked up the phone and started making trades happen.

"What is this guy doing?" was the general line among the partners.

I knew I was doing the right thing, though. My time on the trading floor and my understanding of options trading was going to make this company solvent again. Within a year, I tripled my salary and was back on my feet.

By the fall of 1995, Alicia was pregnant again. We were over the moon happy, but when she went for the ultrasound a few months later, she learned some news that floored me. I'll never forget that day. I arrived home from work, my tie loosened from the day's grind, and she gave me that doe-eyed look like something was wrong.

"What is it?" I asked breathlessly.

"Maybe you should sit down," she said in a gentle tone.

My hands felt numb as I did as she suggested. All I could think about was there had to be something wrong with the baby. But then I saw how her lips curled at the corners, as if she was having trouble hiding her joy.

"Guess what?" she said.

I shrugged, flummoxed. "What?"

"It's twins."

It's crazy to think about this, but my first reaction was to laugh. "Stop kidding around. I'm hungry. What's for dinner."

"No, really," she said with a grin. "It's twins."

We went back and forth like that for a while because I thought she was messing with me. But then I remembered a few lessons I had picked up from Pastor Dan.

"Do you know what the name Joseph means?" he had asked me once after one of his revivals.

"No," I had said.

"It means, 'God will add.'"

I remember laughing. "All I've done is subtract."

But then there I was, sitting across from an increasingly incredulous Alicia who was telling me we were due for not only our fifth child, but our sixth, as well. *This prosperity thing really works*, I thought.

"So it's twins," I said to her.

She held her hands up. "Oh, *now* you believe me?"

I gave her a befuddled little smile. "God will add."

Our twins, who we named Dominique (we call her "Nikki") and Joshua, were born in March of 1996. Our oldest daughter, Alexandra, had turned seven that year, so somehow we found ourselves with six kids under the age of seven. I would go to work while Alicia would send two of the kids off to school and stay home with four of them in diapers. We had so little room left in our house that I would occasionally have to sleep on the floor. There just wasn't enough space in our bed whenever Alicia had to breastfeed during the night. She would have one twin on one side and the other on the other, and this would go on every three hours. Looking back, my wife and I talk about those days often, but neither of us can remember much about them.

It was around that time that it started to become clear to Alicia and me that we belonged more in the revival settings at Pastor Dan's meetings than we did at Christ Community. Alicia and I were doing quite a bit of growing at the revival meetings. They were livelier and more emotional. When Pastor Dan decided to start a church, it was an easy decision for Alicia and me to join. We felt sorry to leave Pastor Cahill and Pastor Ravis behind—they were great influences in our lives—but we just felt like it was time to move on. We had a few meetings with them where we prayed and cried over whether it was the right thing, but ultimately, we could sense that we needed a transition.

That word *transition* would follow me around everywhere I went in those days.

CHAPTER EIGHT

The Watch

PASTOR DAN'S CHURCH met on the eighteenth floor at 90 West Street, just a block away from the World Trade Center. As it happened, the fourth floor of that same building housed the trading room where I worked. The church was called "Faith Exchange," and it grew quickly. We filled 150 to 200 seats, many of the people either direct from Wall Street or on the backs of invites I extended to friends and acquaintances from New Jersey. It was a nice change for us in terms of the enthusiasm we enjoyed from our fellow churchgoers, but the commute to church from home proved to be quite a bit more difficult than the elevator commute to church from the office. Driving into the city on a Sunday morning with all those kids in the back seat was a trip.

Once, we'd gotten all the way into the shadow of Manhattan when Jacqui said, "Mommy, I don't have any shoes." After quite a bit of grumbling and hawing, I found a parking spot two blocks from the church and carried Shoeless Jacqui in for the service.

Other times, someone would get carsick, and we'd have to pull over on the highway to let them throw up. They'd do the deed, get back in the car, and we'd head to church. On more than one occasion, we'd arrive in the city with at least one child who'd wet their pants. It was frustrating, and always hilarious, but we did it every Sunday.

I guess we got so good at driving that zoo of ours to church that people began to notice, because we were eventually offered the position of driving the church bus. They even made Alicia and me elders, even though I didn't really want to be an elder again.

Occasionally, my new position afforded me the opportunity to travel around the country and speak or even preach at different places. Seeing the impact of my words, watching the Holy Spirit move—those were some of the greatest times of my life. People would often tell me that I should make my living as a traveling preacher, but all I could ever think about was getting back to work on Monday because I had six kids and a wife to provide for.

Preaching sometimes put quite a bit of pressure on me because I wouldn't often have a lot of lead time to come up with sermons. Often, I'd get a call on a Saturday night to preach on Sunday, or even a call at work to preach that same night. Without anything specific written in advance, all I could do was pray that the Holy Spirit would lead me through scriptures and give me words to say. The response was mind-boggling. I enjoyed making people laugh, and because I had spent so much of my life hurting, I had a passion for people who were hurting. In many ways, I preached from my pain.

Meanwhile, I would wake up every day knowing that I owed $170,000 to someone I respected. I felt trapped. I made many prayers asking for guidance on how to make it through. The only thing that ever seemed to make sense in those days was to keep preaching with passion.

That point became more and more evident over the year that followed. Between 1999 and 2000, I swung from job to job in Wall Street settings, always gaining a ton at first before losing it spectacularly and having to move on. I was exposed to some shady partners and some questionable business practices, but the thing that bothered me most was how it was becoming increasingly clear that I was pursuing a life and a profession that didn't suit me. I could make big money in short order, but I also had a tendency to lose it just as quickly. The flaws in that ethic were getting awfully heavy for me to carry.

Then, on July 25, 2000, the big one happened, one of the worst trading days I'd ever had. Having lost almost all of what was left of my money, I fell into an immediate and shockingly deep depression. Even in a lifetime that sometimes had taken me to dark places, I'd never been in one quite this dark. Fortunately, I didn't have to travel far to find my way out of it this time. I took the elevator up to Faith Exchange, where I began to pray.

"God," I said, "I don't want to live the way I'm living anymore. It's not fair to my family for me to keep failing like this." The tears spilled over my cheeks. "God, what do you want from me?"

For the first time in my life, I felt like I could hear a response in my heart. The cynical among us might say that I was just talking to myself, but I don't believe that. I believe that God speaks to us through the Holy Spirit, and it's a feeling that we sense in our hearts. In a way, this was my first true heart-to-heart with God.

You're supposed to be preaching all the time, was the feeling.

"Okay," I said. "How am I going to do that? Do you mean I should travel around the country and preach?" This was an overly hopeful thought. This is what many aspiring preachers think about when they first decide to go into the ministry—that preaching will afford them the opportunity to travel the world to spread the Word of God.

Immediately, the answer was, *No. You won't travel. You will start a church in North Brunswick, and there you will preach hope—the same hope you have received here today.*

And it was true. I felt exponentially more hopeful in that moment than I had when I first sat down. At the same time, I held on to that initial objection that I didn't want to be a full-time pastor. I also knew that Alicia would never be interested in being a pastor's wife.

For the next two hours, I just sat there and cried through my conflicted thoughts and feelings. Then, after a time, I noticed a familiar voice on the radio that was playing near where I sat. It was my pastor speaking on the broadcast. The moment I started opening my ears to his message, I heard him say, "Unless you follow your life's true purpose, you will never experience life."

Those words hit me as if they had been spoken to me directly by God. There was no way this could be mere coincidence. This was God's final attempt to get me to see the truth in what He was asking of me.

"Okay then, God," I said. "I'll do it."

And it was like the weight of the world lifted from my shoulders. Even though I had lost all that money and would surely lose my job that day, I had never felt lighter or freer in my life. My life as a trader, church volunteer, and father of six was like the chaos and cacophony of sitting in bumper-to-bumper traffic—all that honking and screeching and bad noise. Then, the moment I decided to become a pastor, husband, and father of six, everything went silent. Calm had returned.

"Alicia," I said as soon as I got home, "God wants me to start a church of our own in North Brunswick."

"That wasn't God talking to you."

"What do you mean?"

"You're crazy," she said. "You need a job so we can feed our kids."

At first, I was put off by the response, but in retrospect, I can't blame her. I could see how, in her mind, being a pastor's wife was like the kiss of death. There's just always so much emotional and social baggage that comes with being married to a pastor—or the child of a pastor, for that matter.

Even though it didn't seem like Alicia had taken me seriously, the next day, I decided to stop trading completely. I handed over what little money I had left in my trading account. With that symbolic gesture, I gave up on the life of trying to provide for myself by playing with other people's money, and instead put myself in God's hands.

That thought made me remember a day not long before that. Back in June of that same year, I was sitting in a church service when they started passing around the collection plate. I felt compelled to give, but I didn't have any money at the time. So I removed my watch and set it on the plate. It wasn't until that moment when I quit my job to become a preacher that it occurred to me what that gift truly meant. The Holy Spirit had compelled me to throw that watch in there "because it was time." It took me over a month to realize the lesson behind the compulsion.

So there I was, freshly unemployed and looking to do God's work. I told my pastor that I wanted to start another branch of Faith Exchange, and that any money we brought in, I would give to the branch in Manhattan. With his blessing, I headed off on the road to build a church.

My first step was to call my good friends Frank and Alanna Stufano, the latter of whom later became our church secretary. Alanna was suffering from depression at the time, depression so deep that she hadn't left her house in a year and a half. Frank was part of a men's Bible study I was leading in North Brunswick, and I would go to his house, where we would pray and try to get Alanna out of bed. The day I called and told Frank I was starting a church, Alanna got up out of bed and said they would both be there. They were all in, my armor-bearers and ushers. Friends Greg and Jeannette Cicio and their family drove an hour and a half from Pennsylvania to help with worship, while John Bevilacqua played keyboard for the first few weeks. We brought in other musicians, too, and everyone was willing to contribute to the growing cause.

I'd like to say that we were roaring successful from the very beginning, but the truth is that we had our first service in the conference center of a Ramada Inn. It cost $300 per week for that room, but we managed to squeak by. It was August 27, 2000, when we held our first service. We didn't advertise, instead relying on word of mouth to drum up interest. That first day, 110 people attended—mostly friends from other churches that were coming out to support us. Ten people got saved that day.

And so it was that Faith Exchange of North Brunswick got up and running. I knew not to expect over a hundred people every week, and it turns out, I was right. By the third week, we were down to only twenty people. The worship team consisted of a guitar player and a piano player. There were six to ten kids in the one room for the children's service, and most of those kids were my own.

Running a church out of a hotel can be difficult. Every time I showed up on Sunday, the lady at the front desk would never remember who I was, and they would constantly switch our room. I would get there at 6:30 a.m. and set up the kids' class and sound system after loading all the equipment into a trailer. Occasionally they would put us in a room with seventy to a hundred chairs, and I would have to rearrange them. Then, once the church was finally set up, I would run home and wake up my family, who took a while to buy into the idea of Dad running his own church. Alicia used it as a kind of cudgel in our relationship. Whenever she was mad at me, she threatened to not attend service the following week. I had to swallow my pride so many times.

Our worship leader, Greg Cicio, would have to drive in from over an hour away, so whenever he was late, I would stall until he arrived. Sometimes I'd have to stall through the sounds of other meetings happening elsewhere in the hotel. All of these difficulties meant that we had a hard time growing in those early days. It was difficult, but I knew in my heart that I was supposed to preach, so I pressed on. I probably preached some of my best messages then, because I was under such pressure. Money was short, and I was still in debt, but when you feel squeezed, you have to cling to the Word God has spoken to you. If you can do that, it's always powerful.

It was about four months into the experiment when we reached our low point. The hotel had assigned us to a room that still had dirty dishes and food left out from the night before. I was way behind schedule on setup already, so I grabbed some tablecloths and just tossed them over the offending tables. I really had to break my back to get things set up in time to wake my family that day. Then, when we returned, there were only three people in the congregation, and one of them was my wife. While I was preaching, one of the other two women in the room got up to leave.

Should I just wait until she gets back? I wondered.

So there I was, preaching to two people—well, really just one person, because I'm sure my wife wasn't listening to me. For a moment, I wanted to cry. But in that moment, I felt the Holy Spirit surge within me once more. "I'm never quitting now," I said into the microphone. Then I started preaching like T. D. Jakes.

When it was over, Greg came up to me and clapped me on the shoulder. He gave me one of those hangdog and yet hopeful looks—I'd been getting lots of those back then—and said, "You know, Pastor Joe, there's no reason to be distraught. All those seats you thought were empty? Those were the ones that had angels in them."

I'll never forget those words. They changed my life. If I'd never heard them, I might have given up one day, but my dear friend Greg gave me an image that I would carry with me forever. There is no reason to be concerned about how many people show up to your service. If you're preaching the Good Word, the message is all that matters.

It was around that time that a massage parlor in North Brunswick was raided by the federal government because they were operating an underground prostitution ring. When the building went up for rent for $2,200 a month, I leapt at the opportunity to redeem the place for the Kingdom of God, even though we really couldn't afford it at the time. Between running up the debt on a credit card and the small amounts of offerings we were receiving each week, we had just enough to cover the rent and a few renovations—a little wall removal and some fresh paint. We managed to fit close to sixty seats in the main room, and we even had two little rooms for children's church, a bathroom, and a storage closet.

That's when those empty seats started filling for us. Not long after we moved into our own proper building, our congregation grew to fifty people. You could literally spit from one side of the building to the other—and I probably did that a few times while preaching—but it felt cozy, and the warmth of the Holy Spirit was very much present. We even had a pizzeria next door for anyone who got hungry after the services.

In our first year as a church, we set up a few ministries and conducted some outreach. This led to more growth for the church, and enough money to keep it running. It was always my intention (and it remains that way) that I would not ever take any money from the church. My role was only to preach. To make a living, I would have to keep another job. These days, that's not a problem, but back when we were first setting up shop, times were tight. By February of 2001, I was down to my last dollar and had to borrow a mortgage payment from my mother-in-law. That was one of the hardest things I've ever had to do.

Alicia and I began to pray for the perfect job to complement my burgeoning career as a preacher. That job came from a start-up company called ICE. They offered me a workable salary and a secure position in finance. The only trouble was the commute. Based in Stamford, Connecticut, ICE represented a two-hour drive each way. Five nights a week, I wouldn't get home until well after 9:00 p.m. Then I'd spend all day Saturday working on my sermon in time for church on Sunday. On Sunday, I would preach from my pain and spread the Word of God.

By the end of 2001, I was doing well enough at ICE to align myself for a promotion to vice president of the company. This led to a nice raise and some stock options, but more importantly, enough money to keep my family going while we built our church.

God's timing is always spectacular. In this case, He was right on the mark with the opportunity to move out of our little rental space, because the fact is we had outgrown it long ago. When a friend found the perfect building for us to move into, I tried a number of angles to get the seller to rent it to us, but they all fell through. Eventually I convinced our parent church in Manhattan to buy the building and rent it out to us, but a snafu with the offer let the building fall to another buyer.

I remember being livid about it—so livid that I decided to take my rage out on the building itself. I pulled into the parking lot in my Honda Accord and proceeded to drive around the building seven times, like Joshua marching around Jericho. After the first three or four circles, I could see some people from the bagel shop across the street staring at me and pointing. I didn't care. I just kept driving and yelling about how this building was supposed to be ours. Each time around, my faith redoubled, and on the seventh time around, I screamed as loudly as I could out my window. Then I felt peace.

A week or two later, I got the call informing me that the other buyer's deal had fallen through. Our parent church snapped up the building, and we renovated the place and got down to renting it from them. By the time we got ourselves set up for the first service, we had managed to squeeze in 140 seats—exactly double the capacity of our old massage parlor rental. The Faith Exchange sign went up in January of 2003, and it was on that day that I felt we had turned a corner toward something even greater than I ever could have imagined.

CHAPTER NINE

Everything Makes Me Prosperous

IN A SERMON, whenever I use the term *prosperity*, the tendency is for the listener to misinterpret the meaning. It's not their fault. It's just part of American culture to hear that word and immediately think of money. The thing about prosperity, though, is that it means so much more than money. This might sound like a convenient lesson coming from a guy whose relationship to money had been so rocky for so long, but it's the absolute truth. Prosperity isn't about financial gain—it's about flourishing and finding success in all those facets of life that make you happiest.

And besides, back when we were still building the church, my family didn't have any money anyway. This is largely because, in 2003, shortly after my revelation about prosperity, I realized that the first step on our path back to that prosperity was to pay off the rest of my debt to Pastor Dan. So, even though it was a huge risk financially, we refinanced our home to raise the money it would take to pay him back. By then, I was so sure that God would provide that it didn't matter how much we were losing by doing this—all that mattered was that we needed to get rid of this impediment to our progress as soon as possible.

There's something to be said for not giving up. Before meeting God, I had given up many times. I almost gave up my life. But here, on the day that I paid Pastor Dan back, I had carried through a determination to its end. I was determined to pay back what I owed, to silence my doubters, and to make my best effort to do the right thing.

Even though we were broke, I still felt prosperous. For the first time in my life, I was excited to wake up every day and get to work. I was passionate about my latest job in finance, but far more passionate about the church project and all the new adventures every weekend brought.

With all our personal expenses, and the fact that I never took a salary from the church, we never seemed to have enough money. I guess that's why, just before the wave started breaking in our favor, Alicia and I decided to take what we called a Local Vacation. Our firstborn, Alexandra, was eleven years old at the time, and on the younger end of the spectrum, our twins, Nikki and Joshua, were four already. That's quite an age range to drive anywhere for vacation, but it wasn't like we had the funds to fly anywhere exotic. So when our vacation time arrived, Alicia and I herded our children into the car and started driving. We didn't even have a specific *direction* in mind as we set out.

After driving for several hours, I pulled up to a back-high-way hotel and rented a single room for the eight of us. I didn't bother telling the kids that what I had actually done was driven in what amounted to a giant loop, and that our room off Route 1 wasn't that far from where we lived. Instead, Alicia and I kept to the ruse each day, driving them around to places we knew they wouldn't recognize and telling them that we'd spend our time in the hotel's pool and the nearby Six Flags amusement park.

Every night, the kids would walk over to an arcade, where they would buy some sodas and pump quarters for hours. Later, after we'd all climbed in bed, or in some cases, into sleeping bags on the floor, Alicia and I would look at each other and just smile. Under the circumstances, it didn't matter what we did with our time, because more than anything, it was great to be together. Better yet, we did it all for a couple hundred dollars.

That would be the last local vacation we would ever take, but in many ways, it's still my favorite vacation memory. It was one of those times as a father and provider that I felt most prosperous. Not even the lack of money could challenge that sense of how right the world was for us.

Then, in 2005, the traditional kind of prosperity leaned our way. My employer, ICE, decided that it was going public with an IPO. By then, I was a senior vice president and held plenty of stock options to make the IPO lucrative enough to ensure my family's financial freedom—that was, assuming everything went smoothly after the company went public.

Those were tough days, filled with internal struggle within the company and within myself. My patience was tested every day, as was my sense of perspective on where I stood within the company. There were days when I would come home so frustrated that I would be about ready to tear my hair out as I vented to Alicia. I remember one day I was pacing in our bedroom and fuming. We had the door closed because the kids were still awake. I'd just gotten home from a long day, and I looked it. My tie hung loosely around my neck, and one look in the mirror let me know that my hair was all disheveled and my skin greasy and flushed.

"He makes me so *crazy!*" I practically hollered at Alicia. I was referring to one particular officer at the company who was against allowing me an opportunity that would ensure financial security regardless of how the IPO performed. At the time, I guess I wasn't yet satisfied with just the *chance* at financial freedom; I had to be assured it.

I'll never forget Alicia's reaction. Around that time, we were learning as Christians about the power of agreement. I'm paraphrasing here, but Jesus said, "When two people agree on something, you can pray together and trust in God to deliver." The notion here is that, when two people pray together, the message is more powerful than when one person prays alone. The deeper message is that the couple that prays together, stays together. This led Alicia and me to develop a kind of catch phrase about how we could pray together to make things happen. The phrase was, "Do you want me to get into agreement with that?" In effect, it meant, "Do you want me to pray with you on this so it happens?"

We used this phrase to help each other find levity in any situation. I'd be going nuts, and she'd be fine, so she would say it. Then she'd be frustrated and I'd be having fun, and I would say it. In this way, we joked around about it often.

So on that day, Alicia had been listening patiently to me for several minutes, and now that I was all red-faced and furious, she cocked her head to one side and gave me an incredulous look. "Do you want me to get in agreement with that?" she asked simply.

In that moment, I realized how ridiculously I was behaving. *Wait a minute*, I thought. *I can't let her get into agreement with that.* It made me think that there are so many more positive things that we could get into agreement with each other about. For a while, I pondered what specifically it was that I wanted us to get into agreement on. And then it hit me: Prosperity was the answer. Instead of agreeing on how people were making me crazy, I wanted to agree about how people were making me prosperous.

"I shouldn't feel this way, should I?" I said.

She shrugged. "I can't tell you how to feel."

"But I shouldn't let him frustrate me like this."

She stood and went to the door, checking to make sure there weren't any children eavesdropping on my meltdown. "You shouldn't let *anyone* frustrate you like that."

"Present company included?" I asked with a half smile.

With the eye roll she gave me, I laughed, and all the frustration rushed out of me in an instant. "They're not robbing us of an opportunity, are they?" I asked rhetorically.

Alicia answered anyway. "You still have your stock, right?"

I nodded. "So I guess the people who are frustrating me aren't really frustrating me." My eyes went wide. "Here's what we can get into agreement on. They're making me prosperous."

It was that day that my personal credo was born. It wasn't just that the officers at ICE were making me prosperous, *everyone* and *everything* was making me prosperous. Even in the darkest, most trying times, what I was really working toward was prosperity. When I write the word *prosperity* here, it's important to note that I'm not writing about money. Sure, one can become financially prosperous, but that's not the only measure of prosperity. Prosperity is advancement—in everything. It's about advancing your life in a positive direction.

It occurred to me after that conversation with Alicia that there wasn't a moment in my life, good or bad, that hadn't led me to this one. Everything I had ever done had advanced me to this point, so everything I had ever done, everyone I had ever encountered, and every moment that felt trying was another moment that made me prosperous. Those horrifying days of my youth made me prosperous. My drug addiction made me prosperous. My failed relationships made me prosperous. My early faults as a husband made me prosperous. My gains and losses as a trader made me prosperous. My struggles to raise a church from the ground up made me prosperous. Even my crippling debt made me prosperous. Everything I had ever done had led me to that moment—to success as a husband and father, to success as a church leader, to success as a businessman, and to being on the cusp of financial success. And everyone I had ever encountered along the way, whether they served as positive or negative influences in my life, guided me toward that prosperity.

"Everything makes me prosperous," I said.

We both smiled, because we knew that this revelation would change our lives. From that day forward, I began living with this new credo in my heart. Every time I faced a difficult trial, I would repeat the words and remind myself that this struggle was for the greater good. And to my great surprise, living under the expectation of prosperity actually *led* to prosperity. I guess it all goes back to that old cliché about the power of positive thinking, but by assuming prosperity, I gained it in every aspect of my life.

When the stock first opened, it didn't perform as well as expected, but my newfound outlook on life told me that if I only stayed the course, all would work out in the end. Two years later, in December of 2007, my stock was worth almost five times the original listing. In fact, I had so much faith in this new perspective that, even while many of my coworkers were selling during the initial window, I was buying. I did this several more times until ultimately selling a good portion of my holdings in 2007. I wound up making more money this way than I ever would have if they had made me an officer prior to the IPO, as I had wanted. It made me realize that the wealth of the wicked really is laid up for the just. And I'm not talking about hundred-dollar bills falling from the sky here—I'm talking about how, if you're a just person, opportunity to prosper will always stand before you.

Financially, anyway, the prosperity had arrived.

I wish that I could say the same was true for the church. While we did enjoy some great positives in 2008, we also saw numerous trials as a church family. The first tragic incident came when my good friend and our worship leader, John, lost his daughter in a car accident. She was only twenty years old at the time, and had just given her heart to the Lord two weeks prior. The young man who was driving her lost control of his car on the parkway. They died when the vehicle rolled and threw them.

We held the funeral at a church near John's house. People lined up for three blocks to pay their respects. John asked me to speak at the funeral, and it was one of the hardest things I've ever done. I had to rely on the Holy Spirit to get me through. But I stood in front of her coffin and gave a salvation message, and twenty-five people gave their hearts to Jesus that night.

A year later, John's wife passed away. I still have trouble imagining how he managed to stand tall through a hell like that. He was such a wonderful person, and if it wasn't for him, we wouldn't have made it as a church. I think that year took a toll on him. He left our church, but he still ministers as a servant of the Lord elsewhere.

That same year, our secretary, Alanna, lost her husband and my dear friend Frank. Frank was with our church from the beginning. He was a rock-solid human being and a beautiful soul, but his health problems were too heavy a burden to carry. At the time of his death, he was in the hospital with heart palpitations. I remember getting a phone call from Alanna on a Sunday morning, saying that Frank had gone to be with the Lord.

"Are you okay, Alanna?" I asked. "Is there anything we can do for you?"

She sighed. "You can pray for us today, I suppose."

"Of course."

"But don't worry about me, okay, Pastor Joe?"

"Well, I—"

"No, I mean it," she insisted. "I'll keep on, because I know Frankie's in heaven, dancing with Jesus."

Despite the weight of the moment, I couldn't help but

laugh at the image. At the funeral, we played the song "I Can Only Imagine," and I could sense that he was dancing, just like Alanna said.

With all the funerals through those two years, we learned as a church how it is to grieve. Personally, I learned that, as a pastor, you have to get used to presiding over weddings and funerals alike. That is a difficult enough concept to face, but when you stand before the prospect of your own funeral, life has a way of delivering perspective.

That same year, I experienced what I would later come to understand was a warning shot from my body. During a quiet evening at home with Alicia, I began experiencing chest pain and shortness of breath. The symptoms were concerning enough that we called 911, and I was rushed to the hospital.

The tests showed elevated troponins, indicating that I had experienced a heart attack. But the next day, they tested again and it was negative for a major heart event. No one on the staff seemed to be able to explain it.

"I guess we should call you the Miracle Man," one of the doctors said. "Whatever these tests are or aren't showing, I suggest you consider this a wake-up call."

After three days in the hospital, they released me with instructions to see a cardiologist and make significant lifestyle changes. I took his advice seriously. I began eating better, exercising regularly, and taking medication to manage my blood pressure and cholesterol. More importantly, I began to view this incident as God's way of getting my attention—a reminder that my time on Earth wasn't unlimited and that I needed to be a better steward of the body He'd given me.

Little did I know that this warning would prove crucial in preparing me for a much more serious cardiac event that lay ahead.

By the next week, I was well enough to preach again, and my sermon was about the power that the devil and his demons possess. "He tried to take us down as a church," I told them. "But he couldn't. And even though it was a difficult trial, we made it through."

Little did I know then that my heart attack would be the least challenging of the demons I would have to face over the years to come. Without that "everything makes me prosperous" mantra, in fact, I'm not sure how I could have made it through with my sanity intact. When the devil hits, he hits hard and close to home. Since being saved, I had always been vigilant, kept a sharp eye out for Satan's work, but nothing could have prepared me for how completely he would try to devastate my family.

It all started in the spring of 2009. Alicia and I were leading a home group for couples at the time, counseling couples with troubled marriages. With my twenty years of marriage experience, I figured I would have something like insight to add to the conversation. So, every week, I asked the group's couples to rate their marriage on a scale from 1 to 10. It always amazed me how even the couples who were openly talking about divorce would rate their marriages so highly.

"This puzzles me," I said to them that day when I saw their latest numbers. "And it says to me that maybe we have a few people not being totally honest with each other here."

At first, I was too focused on reading the expressions of the couples in the room to notice how troubled my wife looked.

"Unless we can confess our sins to one another," I said, "there will never be any healing in our relationships."

Everyone started to nod uncomfortably and exchange knowing looks.

"So we have to make sure we're being completely open and honest," I continued. "Even Alicia and I know how difficult it can be to share our feelings, but that's exactly what we have to do here today. We have to stop pretending and start healing."

The room seemed to breathe a collective sigh. Still, I failed to notice that my wife was among them. I never would have guessed that she was feeling the same way our troubled couples were feeling.

"This is what I want to do," I said. "We're going to go around the circle, and everyone is going to say something honest—something that you have never said before."

The effort went extremely well. Each person in the group had said something that seemed like a major breakthrough. Even as they spoke their words, I could see the catharsis written on each couple's faces. This wasn't the end of their troubles, but it was certainly the beginning of the end.

Then it came to be Alicia's turn, and out of nowhere, she shook everything I understood to be true about our marriage to the foundation. "I've hated you for fifteen years," she said.

My mouth fell open. So did the mouths of several others in the room.

"I'm sorry?" I said, hoping that I hadn't heard her correctly.

She proceeded to rip me apart in front of everyone, listing

all my sins from over the years and all the ways I had taken advantage of her and our family as I focused on my own needs. As I listened, I couldn't help but feel the embarrassment rise to my collar. I wasn't just the leader of this group, I was the pastor of the church, and here she was crushing me in front of a collection of our congregants. Inside, I wanted to lash out—and when she was finished, I did get to vent for a minute—but then I realized that I had to live by what I was preaching.

The rest of that session with the home group became about my marriage and how bad I was and how angry Alicia was and how she didn't like me anymore. It floored me to realize how long she had held me in contempt. When it was over, I was hurt and afraid for our marriage, but more than that, I could see that it had done my wife good to share these thoughts. I couldn't relate to how a person could hold on to so much pain and resentment for so many years, but it was clear that sharing was the first step toward letting it go.

Now that I have the benefit of hindsight, I understand how her reaction and her feelings shouldn't have been so surprising. For one, I had certainly made her endure long periods of my selfish and self-destructive behavior. For another, at the time when she finally made the truth known, she was dealing with some personal demons of her own.

The incident at the couples group had happened just a couple of months after her stepfather died. It's difficult enough to grieve someone who passes, but in this case, the man in question had been emotionally, verbally, and sexually abusive to Alicia. As long as I had known my wife, her stepfather had been the dark hole into which she could concentrate all her hate and anger. So when he died, I distinctly remember thinking that there would be a reckoning of some kind for my wife. All those years of despising someone—now that he was gone, it would free her anger for others. As it turned out, I was the most logical and certainly the most deserving target.

The devil is very precise. My temptations had been many over the years, and my downfalls numerous as well, but there is no way to prepare for seeing what I saw that night when my wife's hatred for me reached its boiling point. When I was still a child, I watched my mother flash a knife at me with the intent of ending my life. Now, in the darkened kitchen of my own house, I watched my wife do the same thing.

The way she looked at me, and the way she was rambling with rage, it was like a different person had crawled inside her skin. Her eyes flickered with madness and fury, and her hands quivered as if she had no control.

Maybe it was the clarity with which I saw the demon that had taken control of my wife. Maybe it was because I had seen something exactly like this before. Whatever the case, even as my wife came after me with a blade, I felt no fear. I stepped aside from her slash and moved to the other side of the room. She glared me down, seething like a deranged cat.

"What's going on, Alicia?" I said as calmly as I could.

She fumed for a moment before turning on her heels and bolting for the stairs. "I'm taking you down!" she called back over her shoulder.

By the time I got upstairs, I found her in the bedroom with the phone pressed to her head.

"What are you doing?" I asked.

She ignored me, her whole body quaking with unbridled anger. "My husband's out of control," she said into the phone. "Please come stop him."

I watched my wife spout more details to the police, but I couldn't reconcile with the idea that this was the same person I had spoken to just that morning. This wasn't my wife. Someone or something else spoke through her that night.

When the police arrived, they came right to me, their posture bent for confrontation. Clearly they expected a man very much off the handle. My guess is that they had seen more than their share of domestic disputes, so they weren't used to the man in the equation keeping a cool head. It likely also helped that four of our six children were at home with us—Jackie in her bedroom, the twins asleep, and Joe there alongside me—and none of them had seen anything amiss.

"I'm telling you," I explained calmly, "nothing happened."

"Then why would your wife call us if you weren't hitting her?" one of the officers asked.

"I honestly don't know why she called. It was like something took hold of her. Like she lost her mind there for a second."

After a while longer of the back-and-forth, they started to understand that I wasn't the unstable monster they had expected to encounter. So they took Alicia into the other room to speak with her alone. I paced the kitchen for a time, trying to put the pieces together and figure out just what had happened to set Alicia off.

The next thing I knew, I heard a small commotion in the living room, and there I saw the officers leading my wife to the door in handcuffs.

"No, no, no," I hollered, rushing toward them. "What are you doing? She didn't do anything wrong."

None of the officers gave a straight answer in reply. One of them held me back as the others loaded my wife into a squad car and roared away with her. As I stood there alone in front of my house, watching the police roll off, I couldn't fathom what could have happened to deliver us to this moment. Our marriage had known its difficulties, but I never imagined it playing out to the theme song from *Cops*. My wife and I loved each other too deeply to fight on this level. None of it made any sense.

They took her and fingerprinted her and booked her. Later that night, I went to bail her out, and as they left, she didn't even look at me. Even now, I'm puzzled about how it happened, but thinking about my wife spending any amount of time in jail is so out of character that it's nearly hilarious. We still weren't entirely sure what the charges would be, but we knew that the prosecutor intended to press charges for something. Filing a false police report was the assumption. Whatever the case, I knew we could get through it as long as we stuck together.

I left my wife to sleep alone in our room that night while I took the couch. It seemed to me that, no matter how any of this happened or why, sleeping next to each other probably wasn't the best idea. When she came down and found me asleep on the couch the next morning, it was like something had snapped. Alicia took one look at me and just started to cry. We had been through our fair share of struggles up to that point, but I had seen my wife cry so few times that it was still a confusing sight to wake up to. She came to me and pressed her head to my chest and cried and cried and cried.

She cried almost constantly for the month that followed. I know that sounds unlikely, but that's how it was. I've never seen anyone do so much crying. It was like she was crying sixteen years' worth of anguish in a matter of days and weeks.

When it was over, we quickly put the incident behind us, and were closer than we had been in years. Even now, whenever we fight, if I let off some steam, she comes right back at me with steam of her own. There's no more internalizing of our struggle. We share openly and honestly. Our marriage has never been stronger.

Unfortunately, the state wasn't as forgiving as my wife and me. When we went to court, we were floored by the charges against her. It wasn't filing a false report. It wasn't domestic disturbance. It was domestic *terrorism*. When the judge handed down the charges, Alicia's crying started up again. I had never seen anything like it. The whole scene was just beyond my understanding. My loving, docile wife had one moment of rage—maybe the only moment of rage she had ever experienced—and because of that, she would face a grand jury.

When we went before that jury several weeks later, they called me as a witness. I can't remember what I said, but it was to the effect of, "Look, if anyone needs to be arrested, it's me. My wife has done nothing wrong. We had a fight. Put me in handcuffs. Right now. Please. Just let her go." The delivery must have been unusual to this group, because by the time I was finished testifying, they were laughing uproariously. That sound was a like a weight lifting from my family's collective shoulders, because I knew it meant that they would drop these ridiculous charges.

The saga came out with a happy ending. That night in the kitchen wasn't our proudest moment as a couple, but so much good came out of it. Together, Alicia and I managed to overcome that demon. Our marriage is now totally healed. We can talk about her abuse from her stepfather now, as well. The whole matter freed my wife in a way that very few things could have. It was her breakthrough, and we're a stronger couple and family for it.

We would need strength for what came next. Any parent will tell you that they can deal with personal challenge and tragedy, and that they can endure strife with a spouse, but when it comes to the child, the heartbreak can be almost too much to bear. My son Joey had been acting out from time to time. He was getting into drinking, and I suspected maybe some drugs. It was never anything more than suspicion, though—at least until the night the police called.

"We need you to come down to the Red Roof Inn," the officer told me over the phone. "We have your son here."

I didn't bother asking what he did, because I already sort of knew. On the scene, we found exactly what I expected. He'd been attending a rave-like party full of high schoolers, all of them thoroughly intoxicated and looking sheepish and afraid. My son didn't share the collective mood of his peers. His expression was rage—that same expression, in fact, that I had seen in my wife that night in the kitchen.

"Let's get you home," I told him.

He stormed past, bumping into me and flying into the back seat of the car. Alicia and I exchanged a worried look before getting in to drive him home. I spent the whole ride trying to get a sense of what would make him think it was okay to do something like that—and I tried hard not to think about the hypocrisy in pretending not to understand how and why a boy so young would turn to alcohol and drugs. But no matter how I questioned him, nothing got through to my son. Joey was like a caged animal, his eyes wild and his hair prickly.

When we got home, he jumped out of the car, bolted for his room, locked himself in, and started screaming about how he was going to kill himself.

Alicia was in tears. "You have to go in there. He sounds serious."

"He's just angry," I said, trying to be reassuring.

But then Victoria, who was standing in the hallway, told me that she had seen him just before he went into the room. "He was carrying a kitchen knife," she said, her eyes brimming with tears.

You don't know the feats of strength you're capable of until you believe your child is in danger. I plowed through that locked door like it was made out of paper.

Now this was my third experience with threats delivered on the sharp end of a kitchen knife, but it was my first occasion to see so much blood. It was the first thing I noticed, the unimaginable depth of blood's redness. The knife lay at Joey's side. The blood spilled from him in great waves.

"Joey, what have you—" I lost my wind as my animal instinct took over. I knelt down before my son, ripped his shirt away, and saw that he had gashed himself so deep and so wide that his insides were falling out. Without hesitation, I pawed for them, trying to push them back inside with my fumbling hands.

There was so much blood. I could feel my wife behind me, crying, but I couldn't hear anything but the sound of my own pounding heart as I tried to put my son back together.

"Please, God, don't let him die," I sobbed. "Take me instead. *Please.*"

While this was happening, someone called 911. By the time the paramedics arrived, my son had lost consciousness. But then when they started to move him, his eyes flashed back open. They didn't carry the same light I was used to seeing in my dear Joey's eyes. They were different. Darker. Not entirely his.

"Kill me," he said in a voice so clear it startled me. "Kill me now."

As the paramedics carted him away, I tried not to think about how this was the same part of the house where my wife had lost herself that terrible night. It was like another entity occupied this room. Like a demon walked among us.

I'm overwhelmed with joy to report that my son made it through his surgery, and the emotional trial that followed. When it was over, he confessed the same sort of anger my wife had shared with me. He resented me for the pressures that came with the work I had chosen. That resentment had built into a ball of anger he just couldn't control. But then we spoke, and then we came to an understanding, and then we both saw each other's pain. We all did some healing, and in that healing, Joey found God in the way I had once found God. He went away to spend some time in a ministry in California, and now he's attending Bible school in Australia with the intention of one day following in his father's footsteps as a minister.

The devil is strong, you see, but he will never be strongest.

This is the same message that guides me now as I lead our church. It is also the same message preached at the rehab center to which I contribute. That rehab center is a particular point of pride for me and its founders—and in many ways represents the full circle of my life to date. I entered my adolescence with a drug problem that stayed with me for decades. I nearly lost a son to drugs. And then, not long ago, I found myself in a position to help a friend open a rehab center that would help other young people through those same problems.

It all started with Joey. As he was making his recovery, we had tried a number of rehabs that just weren't working. That's when I crossed paths with a congregant named Jim Marshall, who had been through many of the same issues with his son. Jim had seen his share of rehab philosophies, and none of them had brought his son success, so now he felt compelled to open a rehab clinic of his own.

"What's missing from the message at all these other places is God," he told me. "You can tell these kids the dangers of drug abuse until you're blue in the face, but until they're exposed to something that can help them fill that hole in their hearts, it's all just words."

We were seated in my office on opposite sides of my cluttered desk. I nodded to my friend and agreed that God tends to be the key component to every message of true import.

"That's exactly why I want to open at this location," Jim said.

"You have a location in mind already?" I asked.

He explained that he had found a broken-down old hotel that would require some rehabbing of its own to get it to where it could house several dozen people looking for treatment. By the time he was finished, I gathered that he hadn't just come to me for advice, but with the hopes that I might contribute financially as well.

"So how much would it take to get the rehab up and running?" I asked.

"About half a million," he said flatly.

"Dollars?" I asked with a chuckle. "Well, that's great, Jim. I'll pray for you."

I could see that Jim was a little dejected to learn that such an investment was out of the range for me, but I could also see that he wasn't going to give up on the idea because he knew it was great and godly. Three months later, he returned to my office and said that he had found an even better place.

"It's on ten acres of land," he said. "The building is five thousand square feet of unused space. It was supposed to be a women's shelter, but it was never opened." He explained that it was in Edgewater, Florida, and while the location wasn't ideal in terms of its proximity to New Jersey, it would be absolutely perfect for his vision of the rehab center. "And we can get it for a song," he added.

"How does the song go?" I asked with a smile.

"Well, we have one week to make a bid," he said anxiously. "But I think we can get it for two hundred sixty thousand dollars."

"And how much of that do you still need?"

He explained that he had taken everything he had—his investments, his pension, everything—and planned to put it into the business, but it still wasn't enough. "Do you think you can help?" he asked.

I could see that my friend believed in this project with his whole heart. God had spoken to him, and it seemed to me that, through Jim, He was also speaking to me. "I'd like to help you," I said to Jim, "but I'll need to see the place first."

We flew down together, and from the moment I laid eyes on the property, I knew that Jim was right. This was something that God was calling us to do. Here we would open a rehab clinic that would help so many young people who struggled in exactly the way our sons had struggled—and in exactly the way I had struggled for so many years.

It was in 2011 that Serenity Springs Recovery opened its doors. I am pleased to write that the company's God-centric message has led to an incredible 80 percent success rate for its clients. Because of my background on Wall Street, I was elected CEO of the operation, but it's really Jim and his son who run the business on a day-to-day basis. I just offer advice when it's asked of me. I like to think that this makes me less the chief executive officer and more the chief encouragement officer. My primary contribution is to speak regularly to the clients about how I was able to overcome addiction through my faith in God. When you have a real encounter with God, as I did, there is genuinely nothing in life you can't overcome.

As I reflect on this season of trials and growth—the challenges in my marriage, my son's struggles and recovery, the founding of Serenity Springs, and my own brush with mortality—I realize that God was preparing our family for even greater tests of faith that lay ahead. The lessons we learned about His faithfulness, about forgiveness, and about the power of prayer would prove essential in the years to come.

We had survived the devil's attacks on our family. We had learned to trust God even when circumstances seemed impossible. We had discovered that prosperity isn't about financial gain but about flourishing in every area that makes life meaningful.

But God wasn't finished with our story. In fact, some of the most profound chapters were yet to be written—chapters that would test everything we thought we knew about His timing, His grace, and His ability to bring redemption to even the most broken relationships.

CHAPTER TEN

Even Her

HOW IS IT that the most unexpected phone calls always seem to come when you're just getting comfortable? I was in the sunroom of my house, that spot where the light hits just right in the afternoon, when my phone buzzed. By 2012, I was so used to the constant ping of calls from church members, recovery clients, and the various people whose lives had intersected with mine that I barely looked at the caller ID before answering.

"Hello?" I said, one eye on a book I'd been thumbing through.

"Joey? It's your mother."

I froze. Twenty-seven years of silence hung between us like a thick curtain. I stood abruptly, almost knocking over my coffee, and walked into the next room. This wasn't a conversation I wanted anyone else to hear—not even the empty walls of my sunroom.

"Mom?" The word almost felt foreign on my tongue.

Her voice was older, of course, but still carried that haunting sort of tone I remembered. "I need your help," she said. "The power's out. Hurricane Sandy."

Like many major events in my adult life, Sandy had passed through with relative kindness to me and mine. We had lost power for a day, had some tree limbs down, but nothing catastrophic. For many in the greater New York area, though, it was a different story. Staten Island had been hit particularly hard.

"Where are you living?" I asked, already knowing I would help her. This wasn't even a question.

"Great Kills," she answered. "Same place I've been for years."

The same place she'd been for years. The same place where, every Mother's Day, I'd show up with flowers, only to have her curse at my children or slam the door in my face. The same place where I'd learned to stand at the perfect distance from the house—close enough to leave the flowers on the doorstep, far enough to avoid the sting when she refused to acknowledge me.

"I have a generator," I told her. "I'll bring it over."

There was a pause, as if she hadn't expected me to agree so readily. "That would be . . . helpful," she said finally.

After hanging up, I stood in the middle of the room, phone still in hand, feeling like I'd just had a conversation with a ghost. Twenty-seven years. Apart from those brief, painful Mother's Day encounters, that's how long it had been since we'd had any real interaction. Twenty-seven years since she'd actively sought me out for anything.

I took a deep breath and went to find Alicia. She looked up at me with a smile in her eyes as I greeted her in the kitchen, where she had already begun to prepare dinner.

"You're never going to believe who just called."

She paused, knife over a carrot. "Who?"

"My mother."

The knife clattered to the cutting board. "Your mother?"

It's difficult to describe how I felt in that moment. The whole thing seemed so surreal. "She needs a generator. Sandy knocked out her power."

Alicia's eyes widened. "And you're going to help her? After everything she's done? Or I guess, everything she *hasn't* done for the past three decades?"

A fair question. Most of what my wife knew about my mother were the stories I'd told her—stories about manipulation and cruelty, about a woman who would threaten suicide in front of her children, who would wield a knife as casually as other mothers might flash a wooden spoon. Stories about a woman who had eventually driven away not just her first husband, but also my biological father, any number of other boyfriends, and then my siblings, and finally me.

"She's still my mother," I said, which wasn't really an answer even I fully accepted in that moment.

Alicia knew me well enough to recognize when my mind was made up. "Do you want me to come with you?"

I considered it, but only briefly. "No, I think this is something I need to do alone."

She nodded, then came around the counter to wrap me in a hug. "Be careful," she whispered. "Not just with the generator."

I knew what she meant. My mother had an uncanny ability to get under my skin, to find the cracks in my armor and widen them with surgical precision. Even as a pastor who had counseled hundreds through their own family traumas, I wasn't immune to the effects of my own.

After loading my heavy-duty generator into the back of my truck, along with some basic supplies like flashlights, batteries, and canned goods, I started out for a place that never seemed possible to visit, at least under cordial terms. I wasn't sure what resources my mother had, and Staten Island had been hit hard enough that stores were likely cleaned out. As I drove, I tried to prepare myself for what was to come. The last time I'd seen her had been the previous Mother's Day. I'd left flowers on her doorstep, as I'd done for years. She hadn't even opened the door.

Great Kills was one of those Staten Island neighborhoods that felt trapped in time. Despite its proximity to Manhattan, it had the look and feel of a small town that had seen better days. As I drove through, I saw evidence of Sandy's wrath everywhere: fallen trees, homes with windows blown out, debris scattered along the streets. Many houses were dark, their occupants either evacuated or, like my mother, waiting in the cold for the power to come back on.

Her house was exactly as I remembered it: a modest, cream-colored colonial with peeling paint and shutters that hung at slightly awkward angles. The small front yard, never well-kept even in the best of times, was now littered with branches and other storm debris. The driveway concrete was cracked and uneven, weeds pushing through.

For a moment, I just sat in the truck, staring at the house. This place held so many conflicting emotions for me, even though it was a house I'd never lived in. My mother had moved here after I'd gone out on my own, but it still somehow felt filled with ghosts from my past. I'd stood on that porch so many times, flowers in hand and sometimes children in tow, hoping for a breakthrough that never came. I'd peered through those windows, trying to catch a glimpse of the woman who'd given birth to me but had long ago stopped being a mother in any meaningful sense.

Finally, I took a deep breath, whispered a quick prayer for strength, and got out of the truck.

The steps to the front door creaked under my weight. Funny, every house my mother had ever lived in seemed to creak in the same way, as if the house itself felt like it needed to protest against her presence. I knocked, three sharp raps that echoed in the stillness of the storm-quiet neighborhood.

The door opened, and there she was.

My mother had always been a handsome woman. Even in my darkest memories, there was a sharpness to her features that commanded attention. Now, she was just old. Her hair remained black as ever, her face lined, her once-straight posture now stooped with age. She wore thick glasses, but I could clearly see those same eyes I remembered—clear, analytical, and distant, as if she were observing me from behind a pane of glass.

"Joey," she said, her tone projecting neither warmth nor cold.

A memory occurred to me then, one I'd forgotten: She always called me Joey when she needed something.

"Hello, Mom," I replied, the word still strangely acidic in my mouth.

She stepped back to let me in, and I entered a time capsule. The smell hit me first, that distinctive blend of cat odor, musti-ness, and something else I could never quite identify. It's funny how smells can transport you across decades. One whiff and I was six years old again, sitting in a house filled with that same scent, wondering why our house never smelled quite the same as my friends' houses.

The furniture was different, though similar—worn, mismatched pieces arranged without a concern for aesthetics or comfort. A small dining table with four chairs sat in what passed for a dining room. Everything was cluttered but not quite dirty, the hallmark of my mother's particular brand of dysfunction. Papers were stacked on every surface, books crammed into shelves and piled on the floor, and there were at least three mugs visible from where I stood, each containing what had to have been days-old tea.

"Electrical panel's in the basement," she said, pointing to a door off the kitchen.

So there would be no time for getting reacquainted. I nodded and went to get the generator from the truck. As I lugged the heavy thing into the house and down the basement stairs, I couldn't help but notice how little my mother had offered to help. No "Can I give you a hand?" or "Let me show you where it goes." Just a direction and an expectation that I would figure it out. Some things never change.

The basement was cold and damp, with boxes stacked against the walls and the vague, musty scent of mildew. I set up the generator and ran the connections. When it hummed to life, I found myself standing there in the basement, holding all the power, both literally and figuratively.

When I came back upstairs, the heater was already pushing warm air through the vents. My mother waited in the kitchen, her arms wrapped around herself as if she still had to fight a chill despite the rising temperature.

"Thank you," she said, and it threw me because I couldn't remember if she'd ever said those words to me.

"You're welcome," I managed to reply.

We stood in awkward silence for a moment. What do you say to the woman who raised you, then rejected you, then called you for help twenty-seven years later? Do you talk about the weather? Ask about her health? Mention the nearly three decades of silence that stretch between you like a wasteland?

"Would you like some tea?" she asked finally, and I nodded, because anything was better than the silence.

As she moved around the small kitchen, I took the opportunity to look more closely at my surroundings. The cabinets were old and in need of paint. The countertops were cluttered with spice jars, mail, and what looked like academic papers from her time at Rutgers. I'm not sure why, but the notion that she might still be involved in some kind of research surprised me.

Then I noticed something on the refrigerator: a pamphlet for a women's shelter held up by a magnet in the shape of a cat. Just as she turned back with teakettle in hand, I gestured to the pamphlet.

"You work at a shelter?"

She paused, then set the kettle on the stove, her eyebrow raised as if she couldn't believe this was news to me. "Actually, I run it. Have for about six years now."

The irony wasn't lost on me. My mother, the same woman who had terrorized her own children, was now protecting women from abuse. *Maybe this is her way of making amends*, I thought. *Or maybe it's just a new place where she can enjoy total control.*

"That's . . . good work," I said, and without meaning it, my tone came out a little skeptical.

If she noticed, she didn't show it. "Somebody has to do it."

The kettle began to whistle, a high-pitched sound that seemed to cut through the tension in the room. My mother poured hot water over tea bags in two mismatched mugs, then brought them to the small dining table. No milk, no sugar, no concern for how I might take my tea.

We sat across from each other, the table between us like a no-man's-land. I sipped my tea, too hot and too early into the steeping process.

"So, you're a pastor now," my mother said, always the one to start a conversation in the middle.

I nodded. "Have been for about twelve years."

"And how is that working out for you?"

There was a hint of something in her voice. Not quite mockery, but close. My mother had never been religious. In fact, she had been actively hostile to faith, dismissing it as a crutch for the weak-minded. To know that I'd found God—or rather, God had found me—during one of the lowest points of my life? My mother would have called it a hallucination or a desperate grab for stability. I called it salvation, but there was no use telling her so.

"It's going well," I said simply. "The church is growing. We're helping a lot of people."

She nodded, as if this confirmed something for her. "You always did like to fix things."

I wasn't sure whether she meant this as a compliment or a criticism, so I let it pass. For a while, we talked about the hurricane, the neighborhood, the general state of affairs in the world—the kind of conversation you might have with a stranger on a bus, polite but impersonal. Neither of us mentioned the twenty-seven years of silence. Neither of us brought up the past.

As I finished my tea, I noticed a framed photo on the sideboard. It was a young girl with straight brown hair and features that reminded me of my mother. I recognized her immediately—Lacey, my mother's surrogate daughter. I remembered her calling out to me from the window years ago on one of my Mother's Day visits. What surprised me was how much she resembled my mother, something I hadn't noticed before. It was almost eerie, the resemblance.

"How's Lacey doing?" I asked, nodding toward the photo.

My mother followed my gaze, her expression softening slightly, but she didn't answer. I decided to leave it alone.

"Do you have any photos of us?" I asked. "Of me, or David, or Debbie? Or the younger kids?"

She hesitated, then stood up. "There aren't many," she admitted. "Most were lost in the various moves. But there might be a box in the upstairs closet. I can look."

I waited in the living room while she went upstairs. The house was quiet now, the only sound the occasional creak of floorboards as my mother moved around above me. I took the opportunity to examine the room more thoroughly.

There wasn't much in the way of personal effects. No family photos on the walls, no mementos or knickknacks that told a story. It was as if my mother lived in a space that could be packed up and left at a moment's notice, maybe a habit left over from our many moves during my childhood. The only thing that suggested permanence was a bookshelf filled with psychology texts, a few of the more prominent bearing titles related to cognitive development and trauma.

A minute later, my mother came back downstairs with a shoebox she set on the coffee table. "This is what I have."

The box was old and worn, with *PHOTOS* written on the side in my mother's distinctive handwriting. When I opened it, the smell of aged paper and old glue joined the omnipresent stench of cats.

Inside were dozens of photos, most loose but some still in the paper envelopes they'd come in from the developer. I began to sift through them, and it was like watching my childhood unfold sporadically, and in reverse. Here was a teenage Debbie. Here was elementary-age David. There were very few pictures of me. Just a couple of faded snapshots where I appeared in group photos with my siblings. Fragments of a childhood I barely remembered. Or maybe I remembered it too well, but only the worst parts. Looking at these photos, you would never have guessed at the dysfunction. We looked like normal kids living normal lives, no hint of the hunger, the fear, the constant threat of violence that had been our daily reality.

"I'd forgotten about a lot of these," my mother said, peering over my shoulder. She reached into the box and pulled out another photo, this one of all five of us kids, me in the middle, flanked by the others. "This was Christmas one year. Harold bought you all presents."

Harold. It had been a while since I'd thought about the man who was the closest thing I'd ever had to a father.

"He was kind to me," I said, trying hard not to tear up.

A quick glance at my mother showed her face was unreadable. "He was a good man. Better than I deserved."

It was the closest thing to an admission of wrongdoing I'd ever heard from her, and it caught me off guard. I looked at her, really looked at her, and saw for the first time not just the woman who had terrorized my childhood, but also a human being who had made terrible mistakes and had lived with the consequences of them for decades.

"Why did you call me?" I asked suddenly.

"The generator," she insisted.

"You could have called anyone for help with something like that. Why me, after all this time?"

She didn't answer immediately. Instead, she carefully replaced the photo in the box and closed the lid as if shutting away the past once more.

"Your sister Karen told me I should call you," she said finally. "I guess I just thought it was time."

"I've been coming to your house every Mother's Day for twenty-seven years," I said, my own voice rougher than I intended. "You could have opened the door at any time."

She looked away. "I know."

"I remember when Lacey called out to me from the window on Mother's Day," I said. "She told me she'd heard about me. What did you tell her?"

My mother's face clouded, if only for a moment. "The truth," she said. "That you were my son. That we were . . . estranged."

"Did you tell her why?" I pressed.

She shook her head. "She was too young to understand all of it. I just said there'd been problems, mistakes on both sides."

I almost laughed at that. "Mistakes on both sides?" I repeated. "Mom, I was a child. You were the adult. You were responsible for what happened to us."

For a moment, I thought she would argue, would fall back on her old defenses and deflections.

Instead, she just looked tired. "I know that now," she said quietly. "I didn't then."

It wasn't an apology. It wasn't even really an acknowledgment of specific wrongdoing. But it was more than I had ever gotten from her before, and something in me—something that had been wound tight for decades—loosened just a fraction.

"I should check the generator again before I go," I said, my voice wavering. "Make sure it's running correctly."

She nodded. "Thank you for coming, Joey."

There it was again, that term of endearment—if you could call it that. Even though I knew that calling me Joey was just another of her tools of manipulation, it affected me in the same way it always had. I went down to the basement, checked the connections, and made sure everything was running as it should be. When I came back up, she was standing by the door, a small, tentative smile on her face.

"Same time next week?" she asked, and it took me a moment to realize she was joking.

Wryly, I returned the smile. "Let's hope the power's back on by then."

As I drove home, my mind was a whirlwind of conflicting

emotions. I had spent so many years trying to forget my mother, to build a life that was defined by her absence rather than her presence. And yet, one phone call, one afternoon in her cluttered house, and it was as if no time had passed at all. The wounds were still fresh, the hurt still raw. But there was something else too: a small, fragile seed of possibility.

When I got home, Alicia awaited me with worry etched on her face. "How was it?" she asked as soon as I walked in the door.

I shook my head, not even sure where to begin. "Strange," I said finally. "Really strange."

That night, as we lay in bed, I told my wife everything—the smell of the house, the few photos in the shoebox, seeing Lacey's picture and how much she resembled my mother, the almost-apology my mother had offered.

Alicia listened without interruption, her hand warm in mine. "What are you thinking?" she asked when I had finished.

I stared at the ceiling, considering. "I'm thinking about forgiveness," I said slowly. "Not just about forgiving her, but about what it means to be forgiven. I've spent my life preaching about God's grace, about how no one is beyond redemption. I've counseled people to forgive those who have hurt them most deeply. And here I am, still holding on to this anger, this hurt."

Alicia squeezed my hand. "It's different when it's your own mother," she said gently. "And what she did . . . those aren't small hurts."

"I know," I said. "But if I believe what I preach, if I truly believe that God's grace is big enough for anyone, then it has to be big enough for her too. And if God can forgive her, who am I to hold on to my resentment?"

Alicia was quiet for a moment. "What are you going to do?" she asked finally.

I turned to look at her, my decision already made. "I'm going to go back. Check on the generator, make sure she's okay. And then . . . we'll see."

And that's what I did. I went back the next day, and the day after that. The power came back on, but I kept visiting. Sometimes we talked, sometimes we sat in silence. Sometimes I brought groceries or helped with small repairs around the house. We didn't talk much about the past. We didn't talk much at all. But something had cracked open, if only slightly.

One day, about a month after that first visit, I said, "David and Debbie—they'd like to see you."

She stiffened. "Why?"

"Closure, maybe," I said. "Or just to see you before it's too late."

She didn't answer, but she didn't say no either, which I took as progress.

It took a year of gentle persuasion before she agreed to a meeting. My older sister Debbie—the one who had suffered the most explicit abuse—was reluctant but eventually agreed. "Just this once," she said. "For closure."

My brother David, who had led me to Christ years ago, was more open to it. "God can change anyone," he said, though I could hear the doubt in his voice.

The meeting itself proved tense and awkward. We sat around that same small dining table, my mother at the head, my sister and brother, along with his wife, sitting across from each other, with me as the mediator. No one knew what to say. My sister kept waiting for an apology that wasn't coming. My mother kept insisting she didn't remember certain events—the knife incident, the suicide threats. My brother, usually so vocal about forgiveness and grace, sat in uncomfortable silence.

The tension in the room was like a lead blanket. I could see it in the way my sister's hands trembled slightly as she clutched her teacup, in the rigid set of my brother's shoulders, in the way my mother's eyes darted and deflected from face to face.

"I remember when you taught me to ride a bike," David said suddenly, breaking the silence. "You ran alongside me, holding the seat, until I got the hang of it. Then you let go, but you didn't tell me. I rode half a block before I realized I was doing it on my own."

My mother blinked, clearly surprised by this memory. "I did that?"

"You were a good mother, sometimes," David said. "That's what makes the rest of it so hard to understand."

My mother looked down at her hands. "I had . . . problems," she said, which was as close to an explanation as she'd ever offered. "I didn't know how to handle them."

"You could have gotten help," Debbie offered, her voice tight with barely controlled emotion. "You were a psychologist, for God's sake. You knew what you were doing to us wasn't normal."

My mother didn't respond, and for a moment, I thought the conversation would devolve into accusations and defenses. But then the mood in the room shifted, not dramatically, but perceptibly. The air felt a little lighter, the tension a little looser. We talked for another hour or so, sticking to safer topics, memories that weren't too painful, updates on our lives, questions about health and work. When we left, my sister hugged me tight and whispered, "Thank you." She never went back, but that one meeting had been enough for her. She had seen our mother—old, frail, and still struggling with her demons—and something in her had healed, if only a little.

My brother went back with me a few more times. He was cautious but committed to the process. And it was during one of these visits, nearly two years after that first post-hurricane meeting, that something remarkable happened.

We were sitting at that dining table again—me, my wife, Alicia, my brother, and my mother. We had been talking about faith, a subject I'd broached carefully over the months.

My mother had shown curiosity, even reading passages from a copy of the New Testament I'd left with her. She had been especially interested in the stories of Jesus's interactions with the marginalized and the outcast. "I think I want what you have," she said suddenly, looking at me. "This peace. This . . . God."

My brother and I exchanged glances. My wife squeezed my hand under the table.

"You can have it," I said simply. "All you have to do is ask."

My brother, the theologian with his master of divinity, suddenly took charge. "It's not quite that simple," he said, his voice serious. "You have to truly repent of your sins. You have to really believe that Jesus died for you. You have to commit to following him. This isn't like joining a club or signing up for a class. This is a total life change."

I bit back a smile. My brother had accepted Jesus at a Six Flags amusement park. The irony of him now placing all these conditions on our mother's salvation wasn't lost on me. The complex theology, the emphasis on true repentance, they were all valid points, but hardly the simple act of grace that had marked our own conversions. My wife's grip on my hand tightened, and I knew she was trying not to smile.

But my brother led my mother in prayer anyway, his voice solemn as he guided her through a confession of faith that was maybe a little more complex than it needed to be. "Lord, I acknowledge that I have sinned against you," he had her repeat. "I have hurt those you placed in my care. I have failed to live according to your standards of love and goodness."

I didn't care about the theological hoops my brother was making her jump through. What mattered was that my mother—the same woman who had tormented me, who had nearly led me to suicide, who had been absent for most of my adult life—was accepting Jesus Christ as her savior.

When they finished praying, there was a moment of quiet in the room. Then my mother looked up, her eyes wet with tears. "I'm sorry," she said, the words seemingly forced from some deep place inside her. "For everything."

It wasn't specific. It wasn't detailed. But it was genuine, and it was more than I had ever expected to hear. My brother, who had been so skeptical, so careful not to get his hopes up, appeared genuinely stunned. Alicia, who had never expected to witness such a moment, squeezed my hand so hard it almost hurt.

"Thank you," I said to my mother, not sure what else to say.

She nodded, then surprised us all by reaching across the table to take my brother's hand. "I'm sorry for what I put you through," she told him.

My brother, normally so articulate and so ready with a theological explanation for every situation, was speechless. He just nodded, swallowing hard.

After that day, things changed. Not dramatically—my mother was still my mother, with all her quirks and defenses. But there was a softness that hadn't been there before. She asked about my children. She listened when I talked about the church. She even, incredibly, came to our house for Thanksgiving in 2016.

That Thanksgiving was like spending time with a version of my mother from a parallel universe. The woman who had once been the central force of chaos in my childhood sat at our dining room table surrounded by stability and peace. Alicia had outdone herself with the meal—turkey, stuffing, cranberry sauce, three different kinds of pie. My children, who knew their grandmother mostly as a figure in stories and the woman who shouted at us from behind her door, were cautious but polite. My mother, for her part, seemed almost painfully aware of her outsider status, of the decades of absence she could never reclaim.

The meal was not without its awkward moments. There were long silences that no one quite knew how to fill. There were references to family events that my mother had no context for. There was the unmistakable undercurrent of shared and painful history that couldn't be glossed over with turkey and small talk.

But there were good moments too. My older son talking about our church. My oldest daughters asking her questions that she at least sounded willing to answer.

Toward the end of the evening, as Alicia was serving coffee and the children had retreated to the living room, my mother turned to me. "I want you to know," she said, her voice low, "that I am proud of the man you've become. Not because of anything I did. But because of who you are, in spite of me."

I didn't know how to respond to that. It was the kind of acknowledgment I had spent decades wanting, the kind of validation I had given up hoping for. Coming now, so late in her life, it felt both profound and hollow at the same time.

"Thank you," I said finally. "That means a lot."

And it did, even though it couldn't erase the past. Even though it couldn't rewrite my childhood or give me back the mother I should have had. It meant something because it showed me that people—even people as damaged and as damaging as my mother—can change. That grace is real and redemption is possible, not just in the abstract theological sense I preached about on Sundays, but in the messy, complicated reality of human relationships.

In the years that followed, my mother and I developed a relationship that, while never warm or particularly close, was at least honest. We had forgiven each other—her for the years of abuse, me for the years of distance. We talked on the phone every couple of weeks. I visited when I could. We acknowledged the mistakes of the past without dwelling on them.

My mother died in the fall of 2020, during the year of COVID. It was a peaceful death, by all accounts. She went to sleep one night and simply didn't wake up the next morning. When I got the call, I felt a complex mixture of emotions: sadness, relief, a strange sense of incompletion. But most of all, I felt grateful. Grateful that we had had the chance to reconcile, however imperfectly. Grateful that she had found peace with God before the end. Grateful that the complicated, painful story of our relationship had ended not in bitterness, but in a kind of grace.

I think about that phone call in the sunroom sometimes. How close I came to not answering. How easy it would have been to say no, to hold on to my resentment, to leave her in the dark and cold. I'm glad I didn't. Not just because it gave me a chance to reconcile with my mother, but because it reminded me of a fundamental truth about grace: It's never too late, and no one is beyond its reach.

Even a mother who once held pills in one hand and a knife in the other, asking her twelve-year-old son to join her in death.

Even her.

Especially her.

CHAPTER ELEVEN

Timing Is Everything

BY 2019, MY life had settled into a rhythm I never could have imagined decades earlier. The church, which we renamed *Grace Church* in January of 2011, was flourishing, with two Sunday services packed to capacity every week. Our congregation had grown from a small gathering in a rented space to hundreds of committed members who called Grace Church their spiritual home. My son had completed a remarkable turnaround in his life, going from troubled teen to ministry college graduate, and was now serving in a role much like an executive pastor and worship leader. And Serenity Springs Recovery had helped hundreds of young men find freedom from addiction.

But anyone who can remember back to 2019 and 2020 will tell you that change—big, sweeping, world-altering change—was coming. Not just for me, but for everyone.

Serenity Springs had been a labor of love. Located on ten beautiful acres with a serene lake at its center, it was just a short drive from New Smyrna Beach. We believed that environment played a crucial role in recovery, that healing happened more readily in spaces that nurtured the soul as well as the body, so the property itself was deliberately designed to feel more like a peaceful retreat than a clinical setting. When we first opened, we had a modest twelve-bed facility, but as demand grew, we expanded to twenty beds.

I'd been drawn to addiction recovery work for obvious reasons. After my own battles with cocaine and the miracle of getting clean without formal treatment, I wanted to offer others the kind of second chance I'd received. But my involvement wasn't purely altruistic. Initially, I'd seen it as a sound business decision as well, a way to do good while also building something of value.

Reality, however, had proven more complicated. Running a rehab facility meant navigating the constant tension between heart and business. We wanted to help everyone who came through our doors, every desperate parent who called, every young person who'd hit rock bottom. To do that, we needed doctors, licensed counselors, support staff, food services, and proper facilities, and all of that required money. More of it than we could have imagined.

On top of this, insurance companies were increasingly reluctant to cover addiction treatment, especially when considering our approach that emphasized spiritual recovery over medication. Our twenty beds suddenly had become harder to fill with clients who had the means to pay for their time with us.

"We're going to lose everything if we don't make a change," I told my partners during a tense meeting in late 2019.

We'd seen so many lives transformed at Serenity Springs. Young men who arrived broken, haunted, and hopeless left with clarity, purpose, and faith. Some even came back to work with us, using their own journeys to help others. The thought of closing our doors felt like a betrayal.

But the numbers didn't lie. Month after month, we were operating at a loss. My partners were resistant to change. They believed things would turn around if we just made the right cuts. I wasn't so sure. I'd seen enough market cycles, enough business failures, to recognize the signs. This wasn't a blip; it was a trend.

In January 2020, I made something of an executive decision. "We have to find a buyer," I told Alicia one evening in our sunroom. That room had become my thinking spot, where the light filtered through the windows in a way that always seemed to clarify my thoughts.

"Who would buy a struggling rehab facility?" she asked, looking up from her book. How many times had we locked eyes in this way? How many times had we walked this road together?

In that moment, something clicked for me. "I might know someone."

The next morning, I reached out to an old colleague from my Wall Street days, someone I hadn't spoken to in nearly a decade, but who I'd seen posting on social media about his own recovery from addiction and how he'd been trying to open a rehab facility in another location. A series of regulatory roadblocks had stalled his dream.

When I messaged him about our situation in Florida, he responded immediately. We had a brief conversation about Serenity Springs—its location, capacity, licensing, and financial situation. I was candid about our struggles but also emphasized the facility's strengths: our success rate, our dedicated staff, and the beautiful property itself.

By that Friday, he was on a plane to Florida. We met at the facility, where I showed him around, introduced him to some of the key staff members, and explained our treatment philosophy. By late afternoon, as we stood by the lake and watched the sun glinting off the water, I could see he was impressed.

"This place is beautiful," he admitted. "But it's going to take capital. It could lose money or break even for a few years, but I have the capital and the time."

"Here, all that work is already done," I pointed out. "The licenses, the staff, the reputation—it's established."

By Monday, he was making us an offer: $2 million for the whole business and property. It wasn't what the place would have been worth in its heyday, but given our financial situation, it was more than fair.

That sounds like a big number in print, but it wasn't the windfall some might imagine. After paying off debts, my three partners and I split a little over $1 million between us. I essentially got my original investment back with a modest profit. But the real victory wasn't financial; it was knowing that hundreds of young men had found sobriety and faith during our eight years of operation.

We closed the deal in early February 2020. None of us knew it then, but we were about to experience one of God's most precise examples of timing I'd ever witnessed in my life.

About a week after the sale, reports of a strange new virus started appearing in the news. What had initially seemed like a distant problem in China suddenly had become a global concern. Markets were beginning to show signs of unease, with increased volatility and downward pressure on prices.

Though we had an investment portfolio, I'd stepped back from active trading by then. After so many boom-and-bust cycles, I'd learned the hard way that my addictive personality could manifest just as destructively in trading as it had with drugs. But on a Thursday afternoon in late February, sitting in that same sunroom, I experienced something I hadn't in years. It was a voice. Not an audible one. A still, small voice that I'd heard only a few times in my life. It happened first before my marriage to Alicia, and then a second time before starting Grace Church.

"Protect yourself," the voice now said.

I was watching the market on my phone, a habit I'd never fully broken. It was about 3:45 p.m., fifteen minutes before market closing. The S&P was already showing weakness. My finger hovered over the screen, and before I could fully process what I was doing, I started buying puts.

For those unfamiliar with options trading, puts are essentially bets against the market. If you buy a put option on the S&P index, you're saying, "I think this index is going to drop in value." If it does drop, your put increases in value. If it rises, your put becomes worthless. It's a high-risk, high-reward strategy that I had sworn off years ago.

I started with a small position, maybe a few thousand dollars. But something drove me forward. My finger kept tapping, adding to the position: $10,000, then $20,000, and finally around $25,000—all in puts that would be worthless in a matter of days if the market didn't drop significantly.

When I finally stopped, I stared at my phone in disbelief. What had I just done? I'd risked a significant chunk of money from the rehab sale, money we needed to live on. I didn't draw a salary from the church; my only income came from investments and real estate. Had I just fallen back into old habits, trading like a gambler?

I went into the kitchen where Alicia was preparing dinner. The aroma of garlic and chicken roasting with potatoes filled the air, the scent contrasting sharply with the roiling in my gut.

"I might have just done something crazy," I told her, explaining how I'd essentially placed a huge bet that the market was about to crash.

She set down the knife she was using to chop vegetables for a salad and looked at me with concern. More than anyone in the world, she knew how trading could consume me. "Please tell me how this isn't like the old days."

"It felt different," I said. "It felt like . . . like God was warning me."

It was an earned expression, the look she gave me. She held it only for a moment before softening. "Well," she said, picking up her knife again, "I guess we'll find out soon enough."

The market closed that Friday with only modest weakness, and all I could do was wait through the weekend, wondering if I'd made a terrible mistake. Then came Monday, and with it, an almost unprecedented market collapse.

As I watched my phone, my $25,000 position ballooned to $981,000. I had to blink several times to make sure I wasn't hallucinating. I'd followed that still, small voice, and suddenly, we'd gained almost $1 million, practically overnight. I immediately took some profits, locking in gains before they could evaporate.

"God was right," I told Alicia, showing her the trading account. "Something big is happening."

That something, of course, was COVID-19. Within weeks, the virus had spread globally, and the world was shutting down. Schools closed. Businesses shuttered. Churches emptied. People isolated in their homes, venturing out only for essentials. The market continued its wild fluctuations, with record-breaking drops followed by partial recoveries.

At Grace Church, we quickly pivoted to online services. I still went to the church building every Sunday to preach, but instead of hundreds of faces looking back at me, there were five to ten people scattered throughout the sanctuary, maintaining careful distance from one another. The rest of our congregation joined via livestream.

It was strange preaching to a camera, trying to project energy and connection into a lens when I was used to reading faces, hearing responses, feeling the energy of a room. But we adapted. In fact, our online audience grew beyond what we'd had in person. People from other states, even other countries, began joining our services. It seemed that in the midst of a global crisis, people were hungry for spiritual connection and hope.

During those early days of the pandemic, I felt a deep gratitude for the timing of the rehab sale. If we still owned Serenity Springs, we would have been facing impossible choices. How do you maintain a residential treatment facility during a pandemic? How do you keep staff and clients safe in close quarters? How do you handle the inevitable financial impact when even fewer people can afford treatment? God had spared us from having to answer those questions. I could only hope that my old acquaintance who had bought the facility would be able to weather the storm.

As the world settled into pandemic life, my pastoral duties reduced primarily to Sunday preaching and the occasional Zoom meeting, I found myself with something I hadn't had in years: time. And with that time, I made a decision that would have seemed unthinkable just months earlier: I went back to trading.

I'd stayed away for years, knowing how addictive it could be for me. But this felt different. The chaos and volatility created inefficiencies that someone with my experience could identify. The market wasn't behaving rationally; it was being driven by fear, uncertainty, and in some cases, boredom, as people stuck at home turned to day trading for entertainment.

From my sunroom, with just my iPad and phone, I began trading again. My approach wasn't about wild speculation. It was disciplined, methodical. I was looking for patterns in a market flooded with inexperienced traders, many using stimulus checks to buy stocks without understanding the fundamentals.

By September 2020, my trading account had grown to where we didn't have to worry so much about money anymore. But now, as COVID restrictions began to ease slightly, Alicia and I found ourselves with a new problem: restlessness. Like so many millions of people across the globe, we'd been cooped up in our home for months, watching the world through screens. The church building was still mostly empty, with just a small fraction of our congregation feeling comfortable enough to return in person. Our children and grandchildren visited occasionally, but always with the awkward dance of masks and distance.

"I need a change of scenery," Alicia said one evening as we sat on the back porch of our home in New Jersey, watching the leaves begin to turn. That autumn was particularly beautiful, but the approaching winter loomed like a threat. Cold weather would drive everyone indoors, potentially worsening the pandemic. And after months of isolation, the thought of being even more confined during winter proved stunningly depressing.

A friend and I had been talking about Naples, Florida, and we'd started calling it "Staten Island South" because of all the New Yorkers and New Jersey folks we'd met down there. "Great weather, beautiful beaches, and no one's as uptight about COVID," he'd tell me during our calls.

I'd always been skeptical about Florida moves; I used to joke from the pulpit, "Whoever moves to Florida always comes back." But with winter approaching and COVID restrictions making New Jersey feel especially claustrophobic, we decided to check it out.

In October 2020, we flew down to Naples and stayed at a hotel—remarkably cheap due to the pandemic's impact on tourism. The moment we stepped outside, feeling the warm sun and gentle breeze off the Gulf of Mexico, something shifted. This wasn't just a nice vacation spot; it felt restorative.

The beaches were like nothing I'd seen before—soft white sand like powder beneath our feet, water so clear you could see the fish swimming around your ankles. The pace of life seemed different too. People walked more slowly, smiled more readily (even behind masks), and seemed less burdened.

On our third day, as we walked along the beach, watching the sunset paint the sky in shades of orange and pink, I said to Alicia, "We should get a place here. Not to move to permanently, but as a getaway."

She nodded, clearly already thinking the same thing. "With what's happening in the market, it might be smart to put some of that money into real estate."

Of course, Alicia could not have been more correct. In a world eager to pivot back to a pre-COVID, in-person reality, real estate was something you could see and touch. The time seemed right to invest.

A realtor friend showed us several properties, but one in particular caught our attention: a four-bedroom in a quiet development called Indigo Lakes. The community featured walking trails that wound around small lakes, perfect for the daily walks that had become our habit during COVID.

The house itself was well-maintained but not flashy. Single-story, four bedrooms plus a den that could serve as an additional bedroom when needed. A modest kitchen that opened to a living area, creating a space where family could gather. A small pool in the backyard, surrounded by a screened lanai to keep out insects—a must in Florida. Throughout the house, large windows let in the abundant Florida sunshine.

"I can see us here," Alicia said as we toured through it a second time. "It feels right."

We made an offer that week, slightly below asking price but not aggressively so. The seller countered, we accepted, and just like that, we were buying a house in Florida. The closing was set for December 28, 2020.

As the date approached, we invited several friends from church to join us for the occasion and help us set up the house. Bob and Debbie, a couple who had been with the church for about eight years, were among the first to accept. Along with our friends Alexa and Marcy, they arranged to fly down with us for what we all viewed as a combination working vacation and housewarming celebration.

After signing what seemed like hundreds of documents at the closing, we received the keys to our new Florida retreat. Our friends arrived throughout the day, and the small group of us spent the 29th arranging furniture and making the place feel like home. Bob and I assembled beds while Debbie and Alicia organized the kitchen. Alexa and Marcy handled living room setup and bathroom essentials. By evening, we were exhausted but satisfied with our progress. The house wasn't fully furnished with all the personal touches yet, but it was livable and comfortable.

We spent the evening sharing a simple meal of takeout, raising glasses in a toast to new beginnings.

"To God's provision," I said, looking around at the friends who had journeyed with us through so much. "And to how timing is everything."

I had no idea how prophetic those words would prove to be.

On the morning of December 30, I woke up early. Debbie had already made coffee. I grabbed a cup, thanked her, and headed back to the bedroom, where Alicia was still getting ready for the day.

Something wasn't right.

"This coffee is really strong," I said after a few sips. An unusual sensation had crept up my chest, but initially, I wrote it off as just another instance of the acid reflux I'd been dealing with for years. I set the coffee aside and decided to take a shower, hoping the warm water would help ease the growing tightness in my chest.

But the discomfort persisted. As I stood under the shower, water streaming over me, the pressure in my chest intensified. It wasn't painful exactly—not the stabbing pain I'd heard others describe during heart attacks—but a heavy, constricting sensation that made it increasingly difficult to breathe.

As I stepped out of the shower and began getting dressed, I noticed another strange sensation: Sweat was pouring from my forehead. I never sweat. Ever. Even during intense exercise. Of course, I'd had that cardiac episode years earlier, and it taught me to take chest symptoms seriously, to never ignore what my body was trying to tell me.

That was when I heard it: that same still, small voice.

"Timing is everything"

Suddenly, a sense of clarity washed over me. Something was seriously wrong.

"Alicia," I called out, my voice steadier than I felt, "call 911."

She looked at me, confused. "What?"

"Call 911 right now," I repeated, more insistently.

She fumbled with her phone, dropping it to the ground in her suddenly shaking hands. Terror does strange things to your head. For me, it took the form of a fleeting, absurd thought: *Is she trying to kill me?* Of course, she was simply in shock, her usually calm demeanor upended by the sudden and emergent threat to my life.

By the time she connected with the emergency operator, I was on the floor in a fetal position. The pain had become something like an office building sitting on my chest. I couldn't speak, could barely breathe. All I could do was curl into myself and pray.

When they heard Alicia's panicked voice, our friends rushed into the room. Bob and Debbie had gone out shopping, but Alexa and Marcy gathered around me with Alicia, placing their hands on my head, shoulders, and feet, praying fervently. I could hear their voices, but they seemed distant, as if I were underwater.

"Lord, we ask for your healing power right now."

"Jesus, protect our pastor."

"Father, send your angels."

Their prayers washed over me, providing spiritual comfort even as the physical pain intensified.

The paramedics arrived, quickly assessed me, loaded me onto a stretcher, and administered nitroglycerin. As they wheeled me out to the ambulance, I caught a glimpse of Alicia's face—pale, terrified, determined.

"I'll follow in the car," she called after me, grabbing her purse and keys.

In memory, the ambulance ride remains foggy. I remember the paramedic asking questions about my symptoms, my medical history, my allergies, but my responses were short, broken by difficulty breathing. The nitroglycerin had helped, but the pressure in my chest was returning. Every bump in the road sent a jolt of pain through me.

The hospital was eerily empty, a ghost town driven by COVID. One overworked person checked us in, and I was wheeled into an assessment room. A nurse hooked me up to monitors while a doctor reviewed the initial readings from the ambulance team. For a moment, as the pain subsided slightly, I wondered if this might have been a false alarm, maybe reflux after all.

As I lay there, a different nurse approached my bed. She was older, experienced, with the kind of no-nonsense demeanor that commands respect. She looked me straight in the eye. "Do you want to die today?" she asked bluntly.

"No," I replied, startled by her directness.

"Then do exactly what this doctor says right now. You're having a heart attack."

Her words cut through my denial, through any lingering hope that this was something minor. I was having a heart attack. I might die today. In this hospital. In Naples, Florida. Two days after buying a house.

The next moments passed in a blur of activity. I was wheeled into a procedure room, where Dr. Gamoris, a thin man with light-brown hair, was already barking orders. A curtain hung between us, but I could still hear the urgency in his voice as he prepared for a catheterization procedure.

The pain had returned full force. The medical team worked frantically, not with the calm precision you see in medical shows, but with an intensity that told me this was serious. As they accessed an artery through my thigh and began threading the catheter toward my heart, everything about the world began and ended with pain.

"Pressure dropping," someone called out.

"I need more light here," the doctor demanded.

"How are you doing, Mr. Adevai?" a voice asked, floating somewhere above me.

"Dying," I managed to reply. "It hurts."

At one point, as the pain reached an unbearable peak, I looked up at the ceiling and surrendered. I closed my eyes and prayed silently.

"Lord, if I die here today, I know where I'm going. I have peace with you. But please, I don't want to go yet. My first grandson was just born. I have my wife, my children, my church. There's still work for me to do."

Darkness. Movement. Pressure.

A strange thing happened next. A sense of peace settled over me. It was unlike anything I had ever experienced before, the depth of it—like a real, genuine peace.

A minute or two later, Dr. Gamoris asked how I was feeling.

"I can hardly breathe," I managed. "The pressure is too much."

And then, suddenly, there was a rush—a sensation like a dam breaking open, blood flowing freely again. The pressure lifted, and I could breathe. The frantic energy in the room subsided as the doctor placed two stents to keep the artery open.

"We've got good flow now," Dr. Gamoris said, his voice relaxed for the first time since I'd first heard it. "How are you feeling?"

"Better," I said, amazed at how quickly the relief had come. "Much better."

The next few hours passed as a procession of tests, medications, and monitoring. Orderlies moved me to a recovery room, where Alicia was finally allowed to join me. I could see she had been crying.

"You scared me," she said, taking my hand.

"I scared myself," I admitted.

It wasn't until the next day, New Year's Eve, that I fully understood how close I had come to death. Dr. Gamoris showed images of my heart before and after the procedure, and the side-by-side was stunning.

"You had a hundred percent blockage in one of your main arteries," he explained, pointing to a spot on the image where the blood flow had been completely obstructed. "If we hadn't cleared it when we did, parts of your heart would have begun to die from lack of oxygen." He looked at me seriously. "Another fifteen minutes, and you might not have made it."

"Timing is everything."

Those words took on new significance as I lay in that hospital bed. If we hadn't sold the rehab when we did, I would have been facing considerably more stress during a pandemic. If I hadn't listened to that prompting to protect my investments, we wouldn't have had the financial cushion that allowed us to buy the Florida house. If we hadn't been in Naples, away from the New Jersey winter, surrounded by friends who could help in an emergency, who knows what might have happened?

Most critically, if I hadn't recognized that voice telling me, *"Timing is everything,"* I might have dismissed the symptoms as reflux, taken some antacid, and waited until it was too late.

I stayed in Florida for the next three months, recovering. The new house that we had purchased as a vacation getaway became my rehabilitation center. Daily, I walked around the lakes in our community, starting with short distances and gradually building up my strength. I lost weight following a heart-healthy diet that Alicia researched and prepared with dedication. I visited cardiologists regularly, took my medications faithfully, and learned to listen to my body in a way I never had before.

There were setbacks. Moments of fear when a twinge in my chest would send me into a panic, convinced I was having another heart attack. Twice, I ended up back in the emergency room, only to be diagnosed with anxiety or reflux. But each time, the medical team took my concerns seriously. "Better safe than sorry," one doctor told me. "Never ignore chest pain."

The most profound change, however, wasn't physical but relational. The night after my heart attack, I video-called my four daughters on FaceTime. As I looked at their faces on the screen, I was overcome with emotion.

"I love you all so much," I told them. "I want to ask your forgiveness for the times I wasn't there, for the times my work or the church or my own intensity got in the way of being the father you deserved."

We were all crying by the end of that call. In that hospital room, staring at my own mortality, I had seen clearly what mattered most. It wasn't the market gains. It wasn't the Florida house. It wasn't even the church, as much as I loved it. It was the people God had entrusted to me—my wife, my children, my grandchildren.

In the months that followed, I had similar conversations with my son, with close friends, with church members I had perhaps been too hard on or too distant from. Near-death has a way of clarifying priorities, of stripping away pretense and revealing what truly matters.

When I returned to New Jersey in March 2021, the church was slowly returning to normal. My first Sunday back in the pulpit was emotional for everyone. I shared my experience openly, telling them about hearing God speak to me and how those fifteen minutes had made the difference between life and death.

"God's timing is perfect," I told them. "Even when we can't see the whole picture, he's orchestrating circumstances for our good. He put me in exactly the right place, with the right people, at the right moment, so that I could be standing here with you today."

Some might call it coincidence. But I always say it wasn't a coincidence—it was a "God-incidence." I've had people ask me if I'm angry that God allowed me to have a heart attack. I tell them that's the wrong question. The right question is: Why was I positioned perfectly for when it happened? Why was I given exactly what I needed to survive financially, geographically, and relationally? Through it all, I saw—and still see—the hand of God moving pieces into place long before I understood the game.

I think often about the nurse who asked me if I wanted to die that day. Her bluntness might have seemed harsh, but it cut through any denial or delay. She understood what was at stake. In life, we often face similar moments of decision—not always as dramatic as a heart attack, but moments when we have to choose whether to listen to that still, small voice or to ignore it and potentially miss God's timing.

My heart attack changed me, not just physically but spiritually and emotionally. I'm more patient now, more present with the people in my life. I'm less driven by achievement and more concerned with relationship. I still lead the church with vision and passion, but I'm more attentive to the individuals who make up our congregation, to their stories and struggles.

And I'm more aware than ever of the precious gift of each day. When you've been told you were fifteen minutes from death, you don't take time for granted anymore.

Timing is everything, as they say, and God's timing is perfect.

CHAPTER TWELVE

The Baby Pastor

I **NEVER SET** out to be the "baby pastor." In fact, when I started Grace Church in 2000, I didn't have any specific vision for what my pastoral identity would be. I just wanted to create a place where people could encounter God and find healing. But life has a way of surprising you, especially when you're following God's call. Sometimes you stumble into the very thing you were made for without even trying.

The year was 2004, and we had just purchased the building that would become our permanent home for Grace Church. I was feeling pretty good about things. The congregation had begun to grow steadily, and after years of uncertainty, we finally had a place to call our own. As a father to six children, having babies wasn't exactly foreign territory for me. But it wasn't until I met Debbie Nannery that I began to understand how deeply infertility could wound a person.

Debbie and her husband joined our worship team shortly after we moved into the building. She had such a pure spirit about her, and she also happened to sing with the voice of an angel, so I came to rely on her as our first real worship leader. She and her husband brought an energy to our fledgling church that made me believe we might actually survive those tenuous early years.

One Sunday after service, my wife pulled me aside. "Did you know that Debbie and her husband have been trying to have a baby for years?" Alicia whispered.

I didn't know, but that information hit me in an unexpected way: It made me a little angry—not at Debbie or her husband or even at God, but at the situation itself. Here was this incredible woman who had given so much to our church, who had a heart of gold, and she couldn't experience the joy of motherhood. It felt deeply unfair.

During our next altar call, I felt a strong prompting to call Debbie down from where she was leading worship.

"I'd like you to come down here for a minute if you would please, Debbie," I said, gesturing to her.

She looked surprised but handed off her microphone and made her way to me. At once, I laid my hands on her shoulders and began to pray. I'm not sure what came over me, but I had absolutely zero doubt that after that prayer, she would conceive. I didn't even think about it; the words just flowed out of me with complete certainty.

Weeks passed, then months, with no news from Debbie. I tried not to let it bother me, but I'd felt so certain. Maybe I'd been wrong. Then one day, Debbie and her husband approached me after service.

"Pastor Joe, we've decided to give up on trying to have a baby naturally," she said, her eyes downcast. "We're going to adopt."

I felt my heart sink a little, but I recovered quickly.

"Absolutely," I said, trying to be supportive. "Please look into it, and if you need a letter of recommendation, Alicia and I would be happy to write one." I paused, then added with complete conviction, "But honestly? We believe you're going to get pregnant. So, uh . . ." I looked down sheepishly. "Keep doing it."

Looking back, I could have worded that last part more delicately. But sometimes the Holy Spirit doesn't care about social niceties.

A week later—the very same week their adoption papers went through—they came to me with news that would forever change the trajectory of my ministry. Debbie was pregnant.

I remember the tears in her eyes as she told me, the way her husband stood behind her with his hand on her shoulder, looking like he'd just witnessed a miracle. Which, of course, he had.

That was the first time I prayed for someone struggling with infertility who ended up conceiving. It wouldn't be the last. Not by a long shot.

Baby pastor is not a title they teach you to aspire to in seminary. And yet, here I am.

It happened so gradually that I barely noticed the pattern forming. After Debbie, there was another couple, and then another. Each time, the story followed a similar arc: years of trying, medical complications, heartbreak, and then—after prayer—conception. It wasn't until people started specifically seeking me out for prayer that I realized something unusual was happening.

"Pastor Joe, my sister told me about you," a woman said to me one Sunday, her eyes glimmering with desperate hope. "She said you prayed for her friend and they got pregnant after five years of trying."

"Are you struggling to conceive?" I asked.

She nodded, tears welling up. "Three years and two miscarriages."

I placed my hand on her shoulder. "It's a done deal," I said. The words came out automatically, and with an authority that still sometimes surprises me.

Four months later, she called me, sobbing with joy. She was pregnant.

After enough of these encounters, people started referring to me as the baby pastor. At first, I laughed it off. But as more and more couples conceived after prayer, I had to acknowledge that perhaps God had given me a specific anointing in this area. It wasn't about me; it was about what God wanted to do through me. And for whatever reason, He had chosen fertility as the channel through which His power would flow most visibly in my ministry.

I've thought a lot about why God would give me this particular gift. Maybe it's because I understand family. With six kids of my own, I know the chaotic joy that children bring. I know the depth of love a parent feels when they look at their child. And I know the heart-wrenching pain of wanting to share that love with a child who doesn't yet exist.

Or maybe it's because I understand what it means to be desperate for something beyond your control. Growing up, I experienced that kind of helplessness far too often.

Either way, I've accepted this calling. It's not one I sought out, and I take no personal credit for the miracles that have happened. But I've been privileged to be present for some of the most profound moments in people's lives—moments when they receive the blessing they thought might never come.

One of the most remarkable stories began with a couple named Alvin and Mitch Bulahan. By the time the two had married, Mitch had already given birth to four children during her previous relationship. Alvin loved those kids like his own, but they both wanted to experience having a child together.

When Mitch finally got pregnant, instead of joy, they were met with devastating news. Their baby, whom they'd already named Matthew, had been diagnosed with trisomy 13, a fatal genetic condition. The doctor told them their son would likely not survive birth, and if he did, would die shortly thereafter.

I wasn't there for that appointment, but Mitch later described to me how she began to cry while Alvin just sat there, staring at a plaque on the bookshelf behind the doctor. When the doctor asked if he understood the gravity of the situation, he recited the medical terminology back to her in a hollow voice: "Trisomy 13. Patau's syndrome. It disrupts development and, in most cases, results in miscarriage, stillbirth, or the baby dying soon after birth. Everything's clear to me, Doctor. Matthew isn't going to make it."

They chose not to terminate the pregnancy. Matthew was born and lived for just a few hours.

Months later, as Mitch was still reeling from postpartum depression, she became pregnant again, only to miscarry. It seemed like having children together just wasn't in the cards for them.

It was during a snowstorm that Mitch happened to catch one of our church's online services. Something about the message resonated with her, and she shared it with Alvin.

"Can we go here sometime?" she texted him. "I think it'd be good for us. Good for the kids."

That next Sunday, they walked through our doors. I didn't know their story then. I just recognized how we had some new faces in our congregation. But God knew exactly why they had come.

After attending for a while, they became involved in our couples group. Their marriage was strengthened, and eventually, they approached me after an altar call.

"Pastor Joe," Mitch said quietly, "we've been trying to have a baby, but after losing Matthew and then the miscarriage . . ." Her voice trailed off.

I laid my hands on their shoulders. "It's a done deal," I told them.

There were complications with the pregnancy. Mitch developed cervical insufficiency, which put her at high risk for miscarriage. Then she developed preeclampsia. But through it all, they held fast to the promise.

Nine months later, I received a call from Alvin. "Pastor, she's here! Marceline Grace was born this morning. She's perfect."

When I visited them in the hospital, the joy on their faces was indescribable. Alvin had transformed the entire floor into a celebration zone. There were dozens of people packed into the room and the hallway outside, pizza boxes stacked high, and in the center of it all, tiny Marceline Grace, soaking up the love.

"I've ordered more pizza," Alvin told me, beaming. "Everyone gets to hold the baby!"

What struck me about their story wasn't just the miracle of conception after such tragedy, but the way they had learned to celebrate with others even during their own waiting period. Mitch had watched her friend Monique (whom I had also prayed for) get pregnant with twins before she herself conceived. Instead of growing bitter, she had rejoiced with her friend.

"Whatever you celebrate, you will appropriate," I often say. Mitch celebrated her friends' blessings, and in time, her own blessing followed.

People often ask me if I believe in coincidences. I don't. I believe in what I call "God-incidences"—those moments when circumstances align so perfectly that you know it can't be random chance. There's a designer behind the design.

Take Manny and Carenny, for instance. Their path to Grace Church began with an Excel spreadsheet sent from thousands of miles away.

Manny and Carenny had one child, and while Manny desperately wanted another, Carenny was hesitant. She had experienced severe postpartum depression after their first child and wasn't eager to go through that again. Eventually, she gave Manny an ultimatum: If he could earn a certain salary by a specific date, they could consider having another baby.

Manny doubled that salary in half the time.

Around the same time, they were looking for a church. When Manny mentioned this to his sister Monika, who lived in the Dominican Republic, she immediately sent him an Excel spreadsheet listing churches near their home in New Jersey. Next to Grace Church, she had added a note: *Look at this one. I like the pastor. He's funny*.

It turned out Monika had been watching our livestreams for years from the Dominican Republic. Though Manny and Carenny had been hoping to find a Spanish-speaking church, they decided to check us out.

After attending for a while, Carenny began talking to my wife, Alicia, about trying for a second child.

That's when Alicia suggested they speak with me. "You need to talk to the baby pastor," she told them.

When we met during an altar call, I asked them what they were hoping to have.

"A girl!" Manny said without hesitation.

I laughed. "Well, in that case, you'll have a girl. It's a done deal." Then I added, "Now, all you have to do is get to work."

They conceived quickly, but their journey was just beginning. Early in the pregnancy, doctors found evidence of a heterotopic pregnancy—an extremely rare and dangerous condition where there are two simultaneous pregnancies, one in the uterus and another outside it.

The Sunday after receiving this frightening news, they were right back at the altar. Our deacons prayed over them, and at their next appointment, the problem had mysteriously disappeared. Doctors weren't sure what had changed, but *we* knew.

All the while, they were hesitant to tell Monika, Manny's sister, about the pregnancy. She and her husband had been trying to conceive for over a year and a half. When Monika visited from the Dominican Republic, Manny and Carenny brought her to me for prayer.

"It is done," I told her, just as I had told them.

Two years later, they received a package in the mail containing a shirt that read, *You're gonna be an uncle!* Monika was pregnant too.

Two done deals for the price of one.

I've seen miracles happen for people who don't even believe in God. I've prayed for skeptics who have conceived despite medical impossibilities. But here's the tragic part: Many of them never looked back. God worked something beautiful in their lives, and they just moved on, never acknowledging the source of their blessing.

It reminds me of the story in Luke's Gospel where Jesus heals ten lepers, but only one returns to thank Him. Jesus asks, "Were not all ten cleansed? Where are the other nine?"

I often wonder about those other nine. Did they go on with

their lives, never giving another thought to the man who had completely transformed their existence? Or did they, perhaps years later, look back and realize what they had experienced?

I don't want to sound bitter. I'm overjoyed for every couple who conceives after prayer, whether they acknowledge God's hand in it or not. But I can't help feeling that they're missing out on the most important part of the miracle: a relationship with the Miracle Worker himself.

One couple who did recognize God's hand in their blessing was Marcela and Alessandro. They had been trying to conceive for seven years—seven years of negative tests, shattered hopes, and growing desperation.

Marcela's life had been marked by loss from an early age. She was born in Ecuador, her parents passed away when she was in her teens, and she bounced around foster homes before ending up in the United States. Just when things were looking up, her guardian died of multiple sclerosis, leaving her alone at nineteen in an unfamiliar country.

She met Alessandro, an Italian from Naples, at a club in New Jersey. They married and built successful careers—she in online direct sales, he as a restaurateur. But something was missing.

After years of their trying to conceive naturally, doctors told them that without in vitro fertilization (IVF), pregnancy would never be possible. They traveled to Ecuador for the treatment, spending $40,000, not counting travel expenses. Marcela was uncomfortable with the idea at first, feeling like she was "playing God." But they went through with it, and to their joy, she got pregnant.

Then, as they flew back over the Atlantic, Marcela began

bleeding. She miscarried on the plane, thousands of feet above the ground. Their final gamble, their desperate swing for the fences—had struck out.

It was a rainy summer Sunday when Marcela came to Grace Church. She sat in the back, finding it difficult to worship. She was at a crossroads: either give up on God, who seemed to have given up on her, or dive deeper into faith. That day, she heard an announcement about an upcoming baptism and decided she would take that step of commitment. Though I had already prayed for her before this, declaring her pregnancy a "done deal," she continued to struggle with doubt and disappointment as the months passed.

On the first Sunday of 2019, I asked the congregation during an altar call to approach the front if they had never felt unconditionally loved by God. To Marcela's shock—and mine—almost the entire congregation came forward.

It was an epiphany for her. She realized that she had been trying to fill the void of feeling unloved with a baby. She couldn't burden a newborn with the responsibility of filling her emotional needs. That wasn't fair to a child.

A feeling like a warm hug enveloped her, accompanied by a peace that made no sense given her circumstances. For the first time, God's unconditional love became real to her. She thought to herself, *Maybe I don't need a baby. Maybe this is all I've ever really needed.*

Later that week, she walked into a clinic with a check in her hand for another round of IVF. But while getting her preliminary blood tests done, the doctors discovered something unusual: She was already pregnant.

Lorenzo, her little boy, was born completely healthy despite doctors' warnings about potential complications. And several years later, Marcela gave birth to a second son, Leonardo.

Her story is a powerful reminder that sometimes what we're really seeking isn't a baby, a job, a spouse, or any other external blessing—it's the unconditional love that only God can provide. When we finally experience that love, everything else falls into perspective.

I've noticed a pattern over the years. The couples who find their way to me often share similar stories: medical complications, years of trying, multiple doctors saying, "It's impossible," and then—after prayer—conception.

But sometimes the obstacles aren't medical. Sometimes they're circumstantial, like in the case of Krissy and Eric.

Krissy had survived an incredibly difficult childhood, yet still maintained a positive attitude toward having children of her own. She wanted to experience the parent-child relationship from the giving end, since she had never really experienced it from the receiving end.

She met Eric at Rider University, and his family provided the stable home she'd never had. Through them, she began exploring faith and eventually became a regular at Grace Church.

Then, in a move that surprised everyone who knew her, Krissy decided to join the Air Force. Around the same time, Eric decided to join the Navy. Their dreams of starting a family seemed to be moving further away. How could two active-duty service members in different branches possibly coordinate having a child?

During an altar call, Krissy approached me. "I just want to have a family," she repeated, her voice breaking.

"Are you sure?" I asked. "Because if we do this, I have no doubt that you will have a baby."

She nodded, and I prayed for her. That very evening, she received her assignment: Air Force security in South Korea, followed by a posting in Virginia. The odds seemed to be stacking up against her.

But then came what I can only call a miracle of circumstance. Krissy was temporarily reassigned to San Antonio—the exact city where Eric was stationed. Although Eric was scheduled to leave the night she arrived, his orders were suddenly delayed. The couple that should only have had a few hours together got two whole weeks. These God-incidences are just as miraculous as any medical healing. They remind us that God is not limited by circumstances. He can work through military bureaucracy just as easily as He can work through human biology.

Krissy returned to Korea pregnant. She spent half her pregnancy there, serving her country even as the baby inside her grew and developed. Just before the cutoff date after which she wouldn't have been allowed to fly, she was processed for return to the US—a procedure that normally took weeks but in her case took just two days.

She gave birth to her daughter, Alba, on American soil, received an honorable discharge, and was able to be a full-time mother.

Sometimes I worry about how much emphasis I place on faith during these prayers. When I tell a couple, "It's a done deal," I'm not just offering encouragement—I truly believe with every fiber of my being that they will conceive. But what happens when they don't?

I've wrestled with this question more than once. There have been couples I've prayed for who didn't end up conceiving. It breaks my heart, and I've spent many sleepless nights asking God why. Why some and not others? What am I missing? I've come to understand that I'm not casting a spell when I pray; I'm submitting a request to my Father in heaven. And like Jesus says, if we who are evil know how to give good gifts to our children, won't our Heavenly Father give good things to those who ask Him? But that doesn't mean He always gives us exactly what we ask for. Sometimes His answer is "no" or "not yet" or "I have something different in mind."

The hardest lesson I've had to learn is that even when I feel complete faith, the outcome isn't up to me. It's up to God. My role is simply to be obedient to His prompting and to pray with the faith He gives me.

This understanding was put to the test in the particularly challenging case of Franceska and Joss. They had been trying to conceive for fourteen months when they first approached me for prayer. I prayed for them, assuring them it was "a done deal." But the months continued to tick by with no positive test.

I would often make eye contact with Franceska during my sermons. Our glances would exchange a thousand words. Mine seemed to ask, "Anything?" Hers would reply, "Not yet."

At the time, Franceska was battling not just infertility but extreme fatigue and depression. During a women's retreat, she confided in her roommate Laura about her struggle. "I'm so tired," she said through tears. "I can't move. I can't think. Every week, I stand at the front of the church and help others get prayed for. I pass them tissues when they cry, hold them up when they can barely stand, and hug them when I know they need it. Every week, I have to put on a face that reminds them to believe. But right now, I don't know where He is."

Laura's response was gentle but firm. "If it's strength you need, you'll have it," she said. "I know the pain of what it's like to see what you see, do what you do every week, and still be waiting on God to show up for you. But there's no chance He's forgotten about you or your baby—a baby who *is* coming."

Meanwhile, Joss was wrestling with his own fears about fatherhood. As someone who had grown up with both a biological father and a stepfather, he worried about measuring up to the examples they had set.

"I fear I can't be both perfectly without sacrificing one way or the other," he confessed. "These great men stand behind me and cast a shadow over all that I accomplish."

Despite these internal struggles, the couple continued to believe. And finally, after seventeen months of trying, on a work trip to Atlantic City of all places, they conceived. Their daughter, Catalina, was born after a difficult delivery that involved multiple attempts at an epidural and temporary numbness in Franceska's left leg. But when they finally held their baby girl, all the struggles faded away.

"Everything makes sense again," Franceska whispered to Joss that night in the hospital.

These stories—Alvin and Mitch, Marcela and Alessandro, Manny and Carenny, Krissy and Eric, Franceska and Joss—they're all different. Different obstacles, different timelines, different outcomes. But they share one common thread: faith that persevered through impossibility.

I mentioned earlier that I've thought a lot about why God might have given me this particular anointing. There's another possibility I haven't shared yet: Maybe it's because I understand what it means to wait for God's timing.

When I first felt called to ministry, I was young and impatient. I wanted to start right away, to build something significant for God. But He had other plans. There were lessons I needed to learn first, experiences I needed to have, growth that needed to happen.

I remember praying fervently for God to open doors for ministry, only to face rejection after rejection. It was frustrating, and at times I wondered if I had misheard God's call on my life.

But now I see that those years of waiting weren't wasted. They were meant to prepare me. God was teaching me patience, perseverance, and most importantly, dependence on Him rather than on my own abilities.

I see the same pattern in the conception stories I've shared. The waiting isn't punishment; it's preparation. God is using that time to work in hearts, to strengthen marriages, to deepen faith, and to prepare parents for the extraordinary responsibility of raising a child.

When Derek and Alexis came to me for prayer, they had been trying to conceive for nearly a year. Alexis had a unique story. God had told her it was time to start trying for a baby, even though she had wanted to wait another year. She was obedient, but as month after month passed with negative tests, she began to struggle with anger toward God.

"I didn't even want a child then," she prayed one day, "but you made me want one, and now you won't give one to me."

What Alexis didn't realize was that God was working on her heart during that waiting period. He was teaching her about unconditional worship—praising Him not for what He gives, but for who He is.

Alexis had received a vision years before where God showed her that her "weapon" was praise—specifically, the Hebrew word *Hallel*, which means praise. But how do you praise when you don't feel like it?

One day, driving in her car, she heard a worship song that broke through her anger and resentment. For the first time in over a year, she worshiped without boundaries, thanking God for all she had even though He hadn't yet answered her prayer for a child.

"When did I allow my soul to grow shy?" she wondered. "When did I forget what I had to be grateful for?"

The next month, she conceived.

When Derek learned of the pregnancy, he was overjoyed. "This is incredible, babe," he said, his voice thick with emotion. "I'm so proud of you."

Their story reminds me that sometimes God is waiting for us to learn a specific lesson before He grants our request. It's not that He's withholding blessings to be cruel; it's that He wants us to receive those blessings with the right heart.

Faith can look different for different people. For Troy and Tatianna, it meant taking their desire for children and surrendering it completely to God.

Troy was in his forties when he met Tatianna, a Russian woman who designed orphanages for underprivileged children in her home country. They married when many said it was "too late in life" to be doing so, and certainly too late to be having children.

They started trying anyway, and after eight months with no conception, Troy got himself tested. As expected, his body was not as primed for fatherhood as it might have been in his twenties.

Troy had learned about surrender from watching his mother care for his father after a brain aneurysm left him paraplegic. She changed the way she prayed, adopting this simple request: "If this is the cross you're having me bear, then give me the strength to carry it."

Troy and Tatianna adopted the same attitude toward their desire for children. If it wasn't God's plan for them, they would accept that and look forward to whatever unique calling He had in store.

It was around this time that Troy met someone wearing a

Grace Church T-shirt at his gym. This led to a reconnection with an old spiritual mentor, who told Troy about our church's special anointing for conception.

Troy and Tatianna came to a midweek service first, just to get a feel for the place. Troy later remarked that if he had felt something *off* with our service, he would have left and never looked back. But they felt welcome, so they returned for a Sunday service and found me afterward for prayer.

Troy was used to long, verbose prayers, so he was surprised—even a little disappointed—by my brief declaration: "It's done."

"It's done? It's done! Can you believe that? That's all he said. He said, 'It's done,' and that was it!" Troy recounted to a pastor friend on the phone afterward.

His friend laughed. "It's done, huh? Well, he called it. If he said it's done, it's done! Somehow, someway, you're having that baby."

And they did.

Troy's story teaches me that sometimes the greatest act of faith is letting go completely, trusting that God's plan is better than our own, even if it's different from what we imagined.

Looking back on all these stories, I'm struck by one common thread: In each case, the couples continued to believe even when circumstances seemed hopeless.

For Patrick and Julie Woglom, this meant trusting God after a devastating miscarriage. Julie had a genetic condition called familial adenomatous polyposis (FAP) that made her hesitant to have children naturally, fearing she might pass it on. But after prayer, they conceived their daughter Madison.

Then, when they tried for a second child, they experienced a miscarriage. It would have been easy to give up at that point, to assume that God had given them one child and that was it. But they came to Grace Church and approached me for prayer.

"It's a done deal," I told them.

A month later, they conceived Mila Grace. The delivery was fraught with complications—Mila came out purple, strangled by her umbilical cord. For a terrifying moment, doctors feared they might lose either the baby or Julie. But they both survived.

Their story reminds me that faith isn't just about believing for the initial miracle; it's about continuing to believe through every obstacle that follows.

Sometimes I wonder if God allows these obstacles to strengthen our faith. It's one thing to believe for conception; it's another to believe for a healthy pregnancy, a safe delivery, and a thriving child. Each step requires renewed trust in God's goodness and power.

As I reflect on my journey as the baby pastor, I'm humbled by the privilege of being part of so many families' stories. I've seen God work in ways that defy medical explanation. I've watched couples who were told they would never conceive hold their babies in their arms. I've witnessed broken hearts heal and faith strengthen through the process of waiting and believing.

But I want to be clear about something: I don't believe God is a miracle-making ATM that we can draw from at any point. Neither do I believe there's anything inherently "more spiritual" about Grace Church, my prayers, or the people in these stories.

These moments of divine intervention are never a reason to boast. They are never to be taken as proof that miracles are guaranteed. I know of several families I've prayed for who didn't end up conceiving. It breaks my heart, but I recognize that when I pray, I'm not casting a spell. I'm asking. I'm submitting a request, in faith, to my Father. And ultimately, it's His decision whether to say yes, no, or wait.

What matters most isn't whether every prayer is answered exactly as we hope. What matters is that we continue to trust God's heart toward us, even when we don't understand His ways.

It's a singular joy, the joy you find in the faces of parents holding their miracle babies. But I've also seen a different kind of joy—perhaps deeper, more profound—on the faces of those who have learned to trust God even when His answer wasn't what they had hoped for.

That's the paradox of faith. It gives us the courage to ask for the impossible while also giving us the strength to accept whatever answer comes. It enables us to declare with confidence, "It's a done deal," while simultaneously surrendering to the reality that the deal might look different than we imagined.

I don't know where you are in your journey as you come to the conclusion of this book. Maybe you're dealing with addiction, as I once did. Maybe you're at a low point in your life, as I have certainly been. Maybe you're struggling with infertility yourself, or maybe you're facing some other seemingly insurmountable obstacle. Whatever the case, I want you to know this: God sees you. He hears your prayers. And He is working, even when you can't see or feel it.

Faith isn't about having all the answers. It's about trusting the One who does.

As a boy, I never would have seen myself serving as a pastor one day. And even after that reality came to be, I never could have imagined being known as the baby pastor. But I've embraced this unexpected calling because I've seen how God uses it to bring hope to hurting hearts.

Every time I place my hands on a couple's shoulders and declare, "It's a done deal," I'm not just speaking to them. I'm speaking to a God who specializes in the impossible. A God who parted seas, raised the dead, and continues to form life in the womb.

I've prayed for thousands of people over the years. Only a small portion of those prayers were about conception. But all of the people who have prayed together with me, I believe, have encountered the living God through those prayers. And there's no greater miracle than that.

So if you're waiting, keep believing. If you're hurting, keep hoping. And if you're doubting, know that your doubt doesn't diminish God's faithfulness.

Because in the end, that's what this is all about: not miracles, but belief. Not conception, but the Creator. Not the gift, but the Giver.

That's the real miracle. That's the done deal.

AFTERWORD

As I've been writing this book, I've been telling anyone who would listen that I was writing this book. I've made no secrets about it, and others have made no secrets about what they thought this book should be and what it should mean. To me, the only purpose for these pages is and always was to give others hope. I've been in dark places—some of the darkest, in fact—but it was hope that allowed me to keep myself moving forward (and alive, for that matter) until my path eventually crossed with God.

Hope is an extraordinarily powerful thing. Even with an absentee mother, no guidance through my adolescence, and a mountain of poor decisions that eventually led me to wanting to take my own life, I found the hope I needed through God. When I first met God, it was the first time I realized that some-one loved me and cared about me. Before then, I didn't think such a thing possible.

That day I first cracked open the Bible my brother had given me, I read a passage that changed my life forever. It was

269

Jeremiah 29:11: "'For I know the plans I have for you,' declares the LORD, 'plans to prosper you and not to harm you, plans to give you hope and a future.'" The notion of a future had never occurred to me before that moment. That passage spoke to me directly. It showed me that, if I believed in God, *anything* was possible.

But I'm a high school dropout, I thought. *I'm a drug-dealing, store-robbing, Rikers-convict, suicidal thinking mess.*

That thought left me with one foot in the dark for a long while after, but the more I lived and learned, the more I learned that hope and prayer and belief can make anything so. If you have the King of the Universe on your side, there is truly nothing you can't overcome.

To contrast where I came from and where I am now, it is clear that my path was nothing short of a miracle. It's still so hard for me to imagine how this can be, but let's run down the list of truths about my present life: I have retired as a senior vice president of a company currently worth $100 billion; I am pastoring a vibrant, growing church where people of all ages are prospering and progressing in every area of their lives; I am the blessed husband of a loving wife, the blessed father of six awesome children, and the blessed grandfather of eleven incredible grandchildren; and I made it through a heart attack. The journey has not been easy, but God's grace has been enough. I still don't believe I deserve this.

From the bottom of my heart, I want to thank you for reading the story of my life, and I want to leave you with this message: No matter how young or how old you are, and no matter what your background, I want you to know that with

God, there is hope, and there is a reason to live. To paraphrase Romans 5:5, His hope does not disappoint. God's hope gives you a future—a future brighter than any you could possibly imagine for yourself. Even a guy like me, a kid with a closed heart, a narrow worldview, and a head full of cocaine, managed to find peace and hope in the arms of God. So no matter where you are or who you are, don't give up. Don't quit. Trust in God, because through Him, something G(o)od is coming your way today.

About the Author

JOSEPH CARLUCCI ADEVAI is the Senior Pastor and founder of Grace Church in North Brunswick, New Jersey. A high school dropout turned Wall Street executive, he retired as a Senior Vice President of a Fortune 100 company before answering God's call to ministry. Pastor Joe lives with his wife, Alicia. They have six grown children—Alexandra, Victoria, Jacqueline, Joe, Joshua, and Dominique—and eleven grandchildren.

www.ingramcontent.com/pod-product-compliance
Lightning Source LLC
Chambersburg PA
CBHW032222050726
47591CB00001B/217